TRACING YOUR FAMILY HISTORY

D0587426

ARMY

compiled and edited
by Sarah Paterson

IMPERIAL WAR MUSEUM

IMPERIAL WAR

MUSEUM

ISBN 1 904 89724 X
2nd Edition
© Trustees of the Imperial War Museum, 2006

CONTENTS

PREFACE

Day in, day out – and for many years past – rather more than a third of all the public enquiries received by the Museum's Department of Printed Books staff have concerned family history. In many cases we answer these using our knowledge of military history and military institutions and with information from our own rich collections. However, we can also provide accurate referral to the many sources and contacts we know, both elsewhere in the Museum and at scores of other specialist institutions and resources far and wide. The details change over time and new sources emerge. We have to keep up to date with these developments if we are to maintain the quality of our service. With the *Tracing Your Family History* series we aim to share our knowledge with you, helping you to find and understand the information that is available. This second edition of *Tracing Your Family History: Army* does just that. It has been comprehensively revised with all the latest information that we ourselves use in our enquiry work.

We are grateful for all the advice and help we have received from Museum colleagues and from other organisations in the preparation of this guide and its predecessor.

Richard Golland
Keeper
Department of Printed Books

ABOUT THE MUSEUM

One of the founding principles behind the establishment of the Imperial War Museum (IWM) in 1917, was its function as a collective memory. Although the original plan for listing the names of the fallen as an intrinsic part of the building never materialised, the Museum has always regarded the individual and his or her experience as being of paramount importance. In his opening address in June 1920, Sir Alfred Mond 'the father of the Imperial War Museum' declared the hope that the collection would be made *'so complete that every individual, man or woman, sailor, soldier, airman or civilian who contributed, however obscurely, to the final result, may be able to find in these galleries an example or illustration of the sacrifice he made or the work he did, and in the archives some record of it.'* Consequently, today we can offer a wealth of material to the family history researcher.

A walk around the main displays on the major conflicts of the century at the Museum in Lambeth Road can help provide a context for a relative's service. There are also additional branches at Duxford in Cambridgeshire, HMS *Belfast*, moored on the Thames opposite the Tower of London, the Churchill Museum and Cabinet War Rooms off Whitehall and Imperial War Museum North in Manchester.

The scope of the Museum encompasses all twentieth century conflict, concentrating on the British and Commonwealth involvement since 1914. In an age of total war, every family in the United Kingdom has been affected in some way. The study of family history, perhaps boosted by the greater availability of information on the internet, has grown considerably over recent years. From schoolchildren interviewing grandparents to local historians writing commemorative histories, the burgeoning growth of this popular activity has made it a real industry. Many of the individuals engaged in research can learn much from the material housed at the Imperial War Museum – original art works and objects of war, personal letters and diaries, contemporary film and photographs, retrospective recorded interviews, and the invaluable collection of printed materials, journals, maps and ephemera. Research may be done in any of the reference departments of the Museum – the Departments of Art, Documents, Exhibits and Firearms, Film and Photograph Archives, Printed Books and the Sound Archive. Access to these collections is both welcomed and encouraged, although a prior appointment is usually necessary. Initial approaches can be made by telephone, letter or e-mail, and staff can provide advice about how to proceed with an enquiry and what materials might be available.

For the family researcher, the first port of call will generally be the Department of Printed Books. This constitutes a national reference library containing well over 150,000 books and pamphlets, 30,000 journals and an impressive range of individual maps and ephemera items, such as ration-books, propaganda leaflets and song-sheets. It is important to stress that the Imperial War Museum **does not** hold any personal service records or official documentation, although through both this booklet and our normal enquiry service, we can offer advice on what and where remaining sources may still be found. We do have a wide range of items in our collections which will assist the researcher. These can all be consulted under one roof, with experienced staff on-hand to direct and answer enquiries.

The primary aim of this booklet is to help the enquirer find out about individuals who served in the Army. Some basic information is given in the following paragraphs, and useful book titles which will help those unfamiliar with the subject, are given in the bibliography at the end. All of these titles are held by the Museum and can be consulted in the Reading Room, but for those unable to make a personal visit, full publication details are given to enable other copies of the books to be ordered through the public library system. Addresses of the various institutions which may assist can also be found listed in Appendix IV.

Strenuous efforts have been made to ensure that the information contained in this booklet is accurate. If any errors have inadvertently been made, we would appreciate it if these could be drawn to our attention so that amendments can appear in later editions.

BRIEF GUIDE TO ARMY STRUCTURE

Before embarking further it may be useful to form some understanding of basic army structure. A soldier or officer would serve in a specific unit of his regiment or corps, and it is important to know precisely with which unit or units an individual served. A regiment is in fact only an administrative formation – it is broken down into a number of smaller units which see active service. An infantry regiment has battalions; a cavalry regiment has squadrons; an artillery brigade or regiment has batteries; and other formations, usually corps rather than regiments, have companies. Infantry regiments are probably the easiest to trace but during the First World War each regiment raised a large number of individual battalions which may all have served in totally different locations. Each battalion would consist of about one thousand men, although for various reasons, the actual number would usually be short of this. It has been estimated that between 1914 and 1918 the British Army multiplied fourteen times in size! Useful books to help understand this very complex organisation are listed in the bibliography – Norman Holding's books are particularly recommended. The web-site *The Long, Long Trail* **www.1914-1918.net** is also extremely helpful.

Please note that the following summary is of necessity very short and is intended to offer a guide to the most common formations only. A fuller picture will be gained by consulting the many helpful books in the bibliography. Readers are welcome to contact the Department of Printed Books for further advice if formations or units are not covered here.

Army regiments are often listed in their Order of Precedence. This means that the regiments are ranked according to their seniority, and dates from previous centuries when regiments were numbered rather than named. (The tradition of named regiments and local affiliations goes back to the Cardwell Reforms of 1881). It should also be remembered that cutbacks in the Armed Forces are not a recent phenomenon, and the size of the Army has always varied according to whether the country is at peace or war. The twentieth century has seen many regimental amalgamations and useful books explaining this are Swinson's *Register of the Regiments and Corps of the British Army* and Hallows's *Regiments and Corps of the British Army*. Another useful publication for those seeking to trace the lineage of a particular unit (i.e. to find out what the unit has evolved into) is Frederick's *The Lineage Book of British Land Forces, 1660-1978*. The constantly evolving web-site *Land Forces of Britain, the Empire and Commonwealth* at **www.regiments.org** is also an excellent source of information.

Photographs can sometimes be of assistance with identifying certain aspects of a uniform, but all too often the photographs are unclear or do not include identifying insignia – cap badges are often one of the most helpful features. Certain factors should be obvious, such as whether the subject is a soldier or officer, or whether he is wearing a uniform for hot climates, but very often the family would know this information anyway. There are books which provide clear photographs of badges and other parts of uniforms which should be of assistance with this. Even if one is able to identify a regiment, this will still not help with working out which battalion or other unit he served with. If the photograph is dated and/or contains the address of the photographic studio, these can be useful clues. For example, if a picture was taken in Dover in 1916, it should be possible to work out which battalion of the regiment was based there at the time. Westlake's book *The British Army of August 1914: an Illustrated Directory* contains an index of locations for units at the start of the First World War.

During the First World War an infantry regiment would usually consist of several different types of battalions; regular (full-time soldiers), reserve (former regular soldiers who were liable to be recalled in an emergency), territorial (part-time soldiers) and service (units raised for the duration of the war). Before the First World War an infantry regiment would usually have two regular battalions – one based at home and one abroad, often in India. The 3rd Battalion was usually a reserve battalion based at the regimental depot. A soldier would undertake to serve 'with the Colours' for a number of years, but after this he would still be 'on the Reserve' and liable to be called up in times of emergency. The number of years varied with different formations, but in the infantry it would normally be 7 years with the Colours and 5 years with the Reserve.

A reserve battalion would not normally go overseas, but would perform the dual function of providing and training new recruits to join other battalions on active service as well as home defence.

In a regiment, there would also be other reserve or service battalions which had been formed only for the duration of the war. After conscription was introduced in 1916, (see Appendix III), these tended to become part of the more general Training Reserve where recruits were not tied to a particular regiment, but were posted where they were needed.

The Territorial Force battalions would usually consist of those numbered 4th, 5th and 6th, and often higher numbers. These consisted of part-time soldiers who had at least had some military training. It was thought that these men would be able to replace the regular units stationed in the United Kingdom and other parts of the Empire, thus freeing fully trained and prepared soldiers to go to the front. The original Territorials were not obliged to serve overseas, but many did sign an undertaking saying that they were willing to go abroad. These units usually formed 1st, 2nd and 3rd line battalions, (originally they were known as Imperial Service, 1st reserve and 2nd reserve battalions) and these would all be in quite different locations. The 1st line battalion (which would be designated, for example, 1/4th) would consist of those Territorials who had volunteered for service overseas. The remaining men would form the basis of the 2/4th battalion – later these units would also usually go overseas. Sometimes, owing to large numbers of casualties or reorganisation, the 1/4th and the 2/4th battalions would combine again at a later date to form the 4th battalion again. The 3/4th battalion would remain in Britain and would provide training for reinforcements to the overseas battalions. Sometimes there were also 4th line battalions, and these would be designated, for example, 4/4th. Some regiments were purely Territorial Force formations, such as the Cambridgeshire Regiment or the London Regiment, which had 88 battalions. Clues for identifying Territorial units include the initials 'TF' in their title, and usually these will be the units which have different line battalions (different numbers divided by an oblique stroke – eg 2/6th or 1/1st). As the 1st and 2nd battalions of a regiment were normally regular formations, if a battalion is designated 1/1st or 1/2nd this means that it was a Territorial unit.

Those who responded to Kitchener's appeal for volunteers formed the New Armies or the service battalions which were often referred to as the 'Pals' battalions. Men from a town or organisation would often enlist and serve together – this would later have a devastating impact on the communities from which they had come. These battalions had higher numbers and often had nicknames such as the 'Accrington Pals' (the 11th (Service) Battalion East Lancashire Regiment) or the 'Stockbrokers Battalion' (the 10th (Service) Battalion of the Royal Fusiliers).

Infantry battalions provided the basic foot soldier who would be in the trenches or front line facing the enemy. The battalion, numbering about 1,000 men, would consist of a headquarters company and four rifle companies, each of just under 250 men. The company would be commanded by a captain and would consist of four platoons each of about 60 men under the command of a lieutenant. A platoon would in turn be divided into four sections of about 15 men commanded by a sergeant or corporal. This structure remained the same but in the Second World War the numbers would be slightly reduced (the battalion would consist of just under 800 men). The size of an infantry battalion today depends on its function, but typically would consist of 600 men or less.

Cavalry regiments were smaller than infantry regiments, containing just over 500 men; these would usually be divided into three squadrons. The Territorial cavalry were yeomanry regiments, and again often there were 1st, 2nd and 3rd line regiments. Sometimes yeomanry regiments were paired and became battalions in infantry regiments.

Both the Royal Artillery and the Royal Engineers have the motto 'Ubique' which means 'everywhere', and hence the information relating to the battery, brigade or company is extremely important. The Royal Artillery is the largest regiment in the British Army, and between 1899 and 1924 it was divided into three distinct formations, the Royal Horse Artillery (RHA), the Royal Field Artillery (RFA) and the Royal Garrison Artillery (RGA). Artillery units were normally broken down into brigades and batteries. Brigades would contain four batteries, and there would usually be between two and four RFA brigades in each division (see below). The Corps of Royal Engineers (RE) performed a wide variety of tasks, ranging from signals, tunnelling and construction, to quarrying and inland water transport. There would usually be three Royal Engineers field companies in a division, and one signal company. In cavalry divisions these were usually called squadrons instead of companies.

Enormous numbers of troops were needed to maintain the Army in the front line, and there were large numbers of men serving in formations such as the Royal Army Service Corps (RASC), Royal Army Medical Corps (RAMC), Royal Army Veterinary Corps (RAVC), Royal Army Ordnance Corps (RAOC), etc. Many of these were awarded the prefix 'Royal' as a reward for service during the First World War. Infantry regiments provided front line soldiers whereas the various corps consisted of specialised troops providing logistical support to enable the fighting to continue. These can prove more difficult to trace than the formations more directly involved in combat. There were a large variety of units of different sizes performing various different functions. Sometimes men from one corps would serve with a different formation – for example an RAMC Field Ambulance (this refers to a medical facility rather than vehicles) would usually consist of about 200 men, but this would include 45 men from the RASC.

Once you have identified the individual's unit, there are generally published sources which can help you find out where the unit fitted into the larger picture. The infantry battalion would be one of four (reduced to three in 1918) which formed an infantry brigade. Three brigades made a division, and they would be supplemented with other useful units from the Royal Engineers, Royal Artillery, Field Ambulances, machine gun units, ammunition columns, etc. Very few brigade histories were published, but most divisions produced divisional histories.

The division is likely to have been the largest formation that a soldier would have identified with. These often had nicknames and formation signs that can help with identification.

The division also served under higher formations – between four and six divisions would serve under an army corps (not to be confused with the various named support corps mentioned previously). The corps would come under the command of an army (there would be three or four corps under an army). Both a corps and an army would have supporting troops, usually taken from the corps or specialised regiments mentioned above under supporting formations – these were often known as 'Lines of Communication Troops', 'Corps Troops' or 'Army Troops'.

During the Second World War the situation remained similar, although the Army was much smaller. Infantry divisions again consisted of three brigades containing three battalions, with the Royal Artillery element of three field regiments plus an anti-tank regiment and/or a light anti-aircraft regiment, and the Royal Engineers element of three field companies and a field park company. There were also armoured divisions, consisting primarily of tanks and armoured vehicles – these really took over the role of cavalry – and airborne divisions. Yeomanry regiments were often converted to artillery regiments.

SERVICE RECORDS

Unless a soldier died in service, it is unlikely that you will find his name listed in published sources (more information about this can be found in the section relating to casualties – if you are trying to trace an individual who died, this may be your best starting point). Commissioned officers are often mentioned by name in regimental histories, and their military career can be followed in the official government publication the *Army List*.

The ranks of commissioned officers in ascending order of superiority are:

Second Lieutenant (2/Lt or 2nd Lt) (sometimes referred to as Subaltern)
Lieutenant (Lt)
Captain (Capt)
Major (Maj)
Lieutenant-Colonel (Lieut-Col or Lt-Col)
Colonel (Col)
Brigadier-General (Brig-Gen) In 1920 this rank was abolished being replaced with Brigadier (Brig)
Major-General (Maj-Gen)
Lieutenant-General (Lt-Gen)
General (Gen)
Field Marshal (FM)

It was common for officers to be promoted rapidly during wartime owing to the high numbers of casualties, and one frequently finds reference to officers holding an 'Acting', 'Temporary' or 'War Substantive' rank. These ranks will always be higher than the actual rank the officer holds – an Acting rank is when an officer is given a rank above his own because of a vacancy. For the first three weeks this would be unpaid, and if it continued for three months for junior officers, six months for lieutenant-colonels, or nine months for colonels, this would automatically become a Temporary rank. A War Substantive rank is a position which the officer would not go below for the duration of the war. If an officer had held a Temporary rank which no longer applied he would revert to a War Substantive rank which would be one grade lower than the former temporary rank. A 'Brevet' rank, which would only be given during times of peace, was awarded to an officer for promotion regardless of whether a vacancy for that rank existed. Although during peacetime he would retain his original rank (for example, captain), if he was to proceed on active service he would automatically become a major with precedence from the date of his brevet.

Men (generically referred to as Other Ranks (ORs) or Rank and File) and non-commissioned officers (NCOs), in ascending order of superiority, are:

Private (Pte)
Lance Corporal (L/Cpl)
Corporal (Cpl)
Lance Sergeant (L/Sgt)
Sergeant (Sgt)
Staff Sergeant (S/Sgt)
Warrant Officer (WO) – class III, II, and I (the rank of warrant officer was first divided in 1915; in 1938 class III was introduced but this was abolished in 1941)

It should be noted that during both world wars, lance corporal and lance sergeant were not a rank but an appointment. It indicated that should a vacancy for the senior position occur, they were qualified and recommended to fill either the rank of corporal or sergeant. There are various grades and appointments for senior non-commissioned officers (SNCOs), and Warrant Officers are usually referred to by their appointment, for example, Regimental Sergeant Major (RSM) or Company Sergeant Major (CSM). However, nomenclature is not the same in all regiments and some use traditional names, for example, a Corporal in the Royal Artillery is called a Bombardier, whilst a Sergeant in the Household Cavalry is known as a Corporal of Horse. Private soldiers sometimes have different titles depending on their branch of service, and this can provide the family historian with some clues. For example, a Sapper (Spr) would have served with the Corps of Royal Engineers, whilst a Gunner (Gnr) would have been with the Royal Artillery. Other examples include a Trooper (Tpr) who would have served with the Cavalry, a Guardsman (Gdsm) who would have served with the Brigade of Guards, and Fusilier (Fus) and Rifleman (Rfn) who would have served with Fusilier or Rifle Regiments respectively (these terms came into existence at different times). Some books, listed in the bibliography, relating to the structure of the British Army will be helpful for understanding more about these different ranks and names.

OFFICIAL RECORDS

The personal service record will probably contain the most detailed information about an individual you are likely to find.

The type of information that these will usually contain are the dates that a soldier served with the Army, the units he was attached to, the dates and a rough idea of where he served overseas, details of his promotions and the medals he was given. Usually some details of hospitalisation or wounds received would be given, and it may contain details about his family, his physical description and any distinguishing marks. Details do vary, and can sometimes be disappointing as the information does not include precise details of where a soldier served or the actions he was involved in. You will need to find this out from other sources, however, the service record will usually be the best starting point and the details contained in this will be the key for further research. The information tends to be brief and will contain many abbreviations – for help in deciphering what some of these might mean, please use the list of abbreviations in Appendix II.

To know where to locate a service record, it is necessary to know the date of a soldier's discharge. **The National Archives, Ruskin Avenue, Kew, Richmond, Surrey TW9 4DU** holds records for soldiers who ceased service before the end of 1920 and officers before 31 March 1922. The National Archives (formerly the Public Record Office) web-site **www.nationalarchives.gov.uk** will prove helpful and includes a very good collection of Records Research Guides (check under British Army in the index). You can visit to do your own research (after obtaining a reader's ticket, for which you will need to provide some form of identification), or they can do the research for you for a fee of £15 per 15 minutes. Alternatively, the web-site has a list of independent researchers who you can employ.

If a soldier served after 1920, or an officer served after 1 April 1922, his record will be retained at the **Army Personnel Centre, Disclosures 4, MP 400, Kentigern House, 65 Brown Street, Glasgow G2 8EX**. If your relative had any service after these dates (for example, if he left the Army in 1919 but served in the Territorial Army during the 1920s or had Second World War service) their record will still be retained by the Army Personnel Centre. There are always exceptions to the rule, and individuals who served with the Brigade of Guards have their records stored in different locations which are detailed in the appropriate section. O41 - 248 7890

PRE-1914 RECORDS

Service records for soldiers who completed their service before the First World War are held at **The National Archives**. The **Imperial War Museum** only covers the period from 1914 onwards and so has very little material detailing pre First World War military history. The **National Army Museum, Royal Hospital Road, Chelsea, London SW3 4HT**, is the institution which covers military history before 1914.

The National Army Museum has a Reading Room which can be visited by obtaining a reader's ticket in advance. They also have material relating to the Army up to the present day, and some regiments have deposited their collections there, for example, the Middlesex Regiment.

FIRST WORLD WAR RECORDS

These are held by **The National Archives**, but it is important to be aware that not all records have survived. Anyone searching for First World War records is strongly advised to read a copy of the publication *Army Service Records of the First World War* by William Spencer. Many records of First World War soldiers were totally destroyed in a bombing raid in 1940, and most of the records which did survive were badly damaged by fire and water. Those that have survived can be consulted on microfilm (the original documents are too fragile to be handled).

There are two record sequences containing First World War service records for **soldiers** (until 1920) held by The National Archives. The 'Unburnt Documents' (document class *WO 364*) consist of about 4000 microfilm reels, and it has been estimated that there is a one in ten chance of finding the soldier you are looking for here. These records consist of duplicate information which was held by the Ministry of Pensions but because they were compiled for administrative use, it is unlikely that they include details of men who died or had no need to claim a pension.

The 'Burnt Documents' can be found in *WO 363*. Although the records are arranged by alphabetical first letter of surname, they are not in proper alphabetical order. It has been estimated that these records form only twenty-five per cent of the original total, but records of both those who survived the war and those who died can be found here.

You will need to know the name, rank, regimental number and the regiment your relative served with. You should be able to find this information from the First World War Medal Index Cards (see the section on medal records for more information about this).

You are more likely to find **officers' records** (to 31 March 1922) as it is estimated that about eighty-six per cent of these are still in existence. There are two sequences to look in and it may be necessary to check both record classes if you are unsure which category your relative would have come under.

WO 339 has the records of about 140,000 men who were mainly Regular, Special Reserve and Emergency Officers (the section on Army Structure explains about these different categories). These are arranged in 'Long Number' order but WO 338 does provide an index for this (for more information about Army numbering systems, please see Appendix I).

WO 374 contains over 77,000 officers' records, mainly for those commissioned into the Territorial Force. This is arranged alphabetically.

POST FIRST WORLD WAR RECORDS

These records are held by the **Army Personnel Centre**, and can only be obtained by written application. Family history research is not especially high on their list of priorities as they are primarily dealing with official enquiries, relating to pensions, welfare, employment, legal matters, etc, and this does sometimes result in a lengthy waiting period. An initial enquirer will receive an explanatory letter and form to be filled in which establishes that the enquirer is, or has the permission of the next of kin. The standard Ministry of Defence fee of £30 is charged for each enquiry.

The Army Personnel Centre will either provide a written summary of the various forms and documents that make up the file or will provide you with photocopies of the contents of the file. As previously mentioned, these can be difficult to understand because they will consist of brief entries with dates and lots of abbreviations that can be puzzling. Hopefully the list of abbreviations in Appendix II will help you decipher these.

You will need to provide the Army Personnel Centre with your relative's full name, and either their date of birth and/or their Army number before the information can be accessed.

BRIGADE OF GUARDS

Inevitably, there are some exceptions to the rule and the Brigade of Guards have traditionally retained their own records. The addresses to apply to for other ranks' records are as follows: **Regimental Headquarters Grenadier Guards / Coldstream Guards / Scots Guards / Irish Guards / Welsh Guards, Wellington Barracks, Birdcage Walk, London SW1E 6HQ**. Officers' records are held either by **The National Archives** or the **Army Personnel Centre**.

THE ARMY LIST

The *Army List* was first published in 1754, and both the **National Army Museum** and **The National Archives** have sets dating back this far. The Department of Printed Books at the **Imperial War Museum** has a virtually complete set from 1914 to date.

This will assist you to trace the service of commissioned officers in the Army (there is no comparable listing for other ranks), but it will be necessary to know the full name of the person you are researching. Surnames and initials of first names appear in the index at the back of the volume, from where one is referred to a column in the volume, under the unit that the officer was serving with. During both world wars these volumes became very large (in the First World War they were published every month), and as many people with the same name were often listed it can be difficult to be sure that you have the correct man. The type of information that can be found in this includes the unit an individual served with and the date of the promotion to the rank he holds – by looking in earlier and later issues it is possible to compile a profile of his service.

Some special issues of the *Army List* do provide more information – for example, *Half-Yearly* or *Gradation Lists*. However, these will only provide the details of Regular Army officers rather than officers of the Territorial Army or those with an emergency commission. An example of this is the January 1946 *Half-Yearly Army List* which includes the full name of the officer, his date of birth, his units, appointments and appropriate dates, as well as details of decorations or awards.

The Department of Printed Books also holds some *Quarterly Army Lists* and supplements from 1918 to 1941 which provide brief histories, not always including the full first name of the officer. We also have some *Gradation Lists* for the years between 1953 and 1968.

If the officer served as part of the British Army in India (as opposed to being an officer in the Indian Army) it is also worth checking in the *Indian Army List* as it provides more information than its British counterpart. We have a complete set from 1914-1947.

There are also a number of published listings of officers serving with particular regiments, although these tend to be Regular officers who made a career in the Army, rather than those who just served during times of war. Examples include listings for medical officers and the Black Watch – you can find full details of these in the Department of Printed Books library catalogue, which can be found online at **www.iwmcollections.org.uk**

MEDAL RECORDS

Campaign medals are given to soldiers who were eligible for them because they served in a particular theatre of war within given dates. Details about these medals can be found in the books listed in the reading list. Some technical terms that might prove helpful when reading through this section include definitions for 'clasp' and 'bar'. Both refer to a narrow metal strip worn on the medal ribbon, but a bar denotes a second award for gallant or distinguished service (and a bar can be given for each subsequent award) – the term bar should therefore only be used in connection with gallantry medals. The term clasp is used in the context of campaign medals, where it will usually include some description, eg '5th Aug - 22nd Nov 1914', 'Burma' or 'Palestine 1945-48'. The word clasp is also used to denote second or subsequent awards of Long Service and Good Conduct Medals or Territorial decorations. The term 'obverse' refers to the front of the medal or the side bearing the principal design, whilst the 'reverse' is the subordinate side of the medal.

FIRST WORLD WAR

The First World War campaign medals are described in detail on the **Imperial War Museum** web-site at **http://collections.iwm.org.uk/server/show/ConWebDoc.986**

First World War medals are useful for the family historian because they do usually include the name and some unit details of the man they were issued to (engraved on the back of the 1914 and 1914-15 Stars, and around the rim of the British War

Medal and Victory Medal). A useful book for deciphering the initials on medals, and general advice is *Collecting and Researching the Campaign Medals of the Great War* by HJ Williamson.

The National Archives holds the First World War Medal Roll (*WO 329*), and this can be accessed by using the Medal Index Cards (*WO 372*). This provides an alphabetical list of those who qualified for the 1914 Star, 1914-15 Star, British War Medal, Victory Medal, Territorial Force War Medal and/or the Silver War Badge. This should provide some basic details of a soldier's service even if his service record was destroyed. The index cards can now be viewed online at **www.nationalarchives.gov.uk/documentsonline/** You can search the index for free, and this will provide you with the name, corps or regiment, regimental number and rank. When you have the right man (or have narrowed your search to a few likely candidates) you can order a digitised image of the medal index card for £3.50 (correct price at time of going to press).

The 1914 Star often known as the 'Mons Star', is a bronze crowned four-pointed star with two crossed swords and a wreath of oak leaves. A scroll reads '1914', with 'Aug' and 'Nov' above and below this. The ribbon is red, white and blue silk, shaded and watered. It was awarded to those who had served in Belgium or France between 5 August and midnight on 22 November 1914. A clasp or bar with the inscription '5th Aug - 22nd Nov 1914' was issued to those who had served under fire between those dates. The majority of men who received this medal would have been Regular soldiers before the outbreak of war (the 'Old Contemptibles'), and recipients would always also have received the British War Medal and Victory Medal. The three medals were often known by the nickname of 'Pip, Squeak and Wilfred', a trio of popular cartoon characters in the *Daily Mail*.

The 1914-15 Star is very similar to the 1914 Star except that the central scroll has been replaced with '1914-15', and the words 'Aug' and 'Nov' omitted. It was awarded to those who had been on active service in any theatre of war between 4 August 1914 and 31 December 1915, unless they were already eligible for the 1914 Star.

The British War Medal was struck in silver and bronze (this latter metal was issued to non-Europeans serving in units of the Labour Corps). The medal features the coinage head of King George V, with a naked man on horseback on the reverse trampling on the eagle shield of the central powers and the symbols of death. The sun, symbolic of victory, rises above, and around the edge are the dates '1914' and '1918'. The silk ribbon has a central vertical stripe of gold with stripes of white and black at each side and borders of royal blue. The medal was awarded to those who had entered a theatre of war on duty or rendered approved service overseas between 5 August 1914 and 11 November 1918. It also covered service in Russia between 1919 and 1920. The British War Medal could be awarded on its own, and was often the single medal awarded to men who served in India during the war.

The Victory Medal in yellow bronze features the goddess of Victory, Athene Nike, on the obverse and the inscription 'The Great War for civilisation 1914-1919' on the reverse. The silk ribbon is a watered rainbow design with red in the centre.

It was awarded to those who served in a theatre of war between 5 August 1914 and 11 November 1918. It was never awarded by itself, and when the Victory Medal and British War Medal were issued together they were often known as 'Mutt and Jeff'.

The Territorial Force War Medal 1914-19 is bronze with the coinage head of King George V on the obverse and has 'Territorial War Medal' around the top. The text 'For Voluntary Service Overseas 1914-19' is enclosed in a wreath. The ribbon is of watered yellow silk with two green vertical stripes. This medal was awarded to members of the Territorial Force who were members on 4 August 1914 or who had previously served four years and rejoined on or before 30 September 1914. They also had to have served outside the United Kingdom between 4 August 1914 and 11 November 1918, and not have been eligible for the 1914 or 1914-15 Stars.

The Silver War Badge is circular and contains the inscription 'For King and Empire' and 'Services Rendered'. It was issued to those who retired or were discharged owing to wounds, ill health or having reached the age of 51. It was first issued in 1916 and continued until 1920.

SECOND WORLD WAR

Second World War campaign medals were not stamped with the holder's name and unit as an economy measure, although arrangements could be made to have this done privately. Eight bronze six-pointed stars were issued, each with the crowned royal cipher reading 'GRI' with 'VI' below. The title of the medal encircles this with the points of the star protruding behind. A maximum of five stars could be awarded to a single person, and if they qualified for more, a clasp could be attached to the ribbon of the appropriate star (the medal for which they first qualified). The ribbons were personally designed by King George VI and all have symbolic significance.

The 1939-45 Star has a ribbon which contains equal stripes of dark blue, red and light blue representing the Royal Navy and Merchant Navy, Army and Royal Air Force. It was awarded for six months service between 3 September 1939 and 15 August 1945. Those who were wounded, captured or died also qualified, and there were other circumstances in which the minimum time period could be shortened.

The Africa Star has a buff or sand coloured ribbon with a wide red central stripe bordered by a dark blue and light blue stripe, representing the desert, the Army, Royal Navy and Royal Air Force. Three clasps could also be issued; '8th Army', '1st Army' and 'North Africa 1942-43'. The Africa Star was awarded for one or more days' service in North or East Africa between 10 June 1940 and 12 May 1943.

The Pacific Star has a ribbon of dark green, representing the jungle, with a central yellow stripe representing beaches, and narrow dark and light blue stripes with wider red stripes at the edges. It was awarded for service in Hong Kong, China and Malaya between 8 December 1941 and 2 September 1945. Service in Burma was excluded, although if an individual was eligible for both Stars, a 'Burma' clasp could be worn.

The ribbon of the Burma Star has three equal bands of dark blue, red and dark blue. The dark blue bands contain a central stripe of orange, which represents the sun. It was awarded for service in Burma between 11 December 1941 and 2 September 1945. Service in Bengal and Assam was also eligible, as was service in China and Malaya between 16 February 1942 and 2 September 1945. A 'Pacific' clasp was also issued.

The Italy Star ribbon contains the Italian national colours in a red, white, green, white and red sequence. It was awarded for operational service in Italy and Sicily (also Greece, Corsica, the Aegean, Dodecanese islands, Yugoslavia, Sardinia and Elba) between 11 June 1943 and 8 May 1945.

The France and Germany Star has a ribbon of five stripes of blue, white, red, white and blue, representing the national colours of the United Kingdom, France and the Netherlands. It was awarded for service between 6 June 1944 and 8 May 1945 in France, Belgium, the Netherlands and Germany.

Two other Stars were issued, which were unlikely to have been given to Army personnel: the Air Crew Europe Star and the Atlantic Star. This latter medal was awarded to members of the Royal Artillery who served on Defensive Equipped Merchant Ships (DEMS).

The Defence Medal is made of cupro-nickel with the uncrowned head of King George VI on the obverse, and two lions flanking a crowned oak sapling on top of wavy lines representing the sea, on the reverse. The date '1939' appears at top left and '1945' appears at top right, and 'The Defence Medal' appears at the bottom. The ribbon has two wide stripes of green signifying the countryside with two narrow black stripes representing the blackout and a wide central stripe of orange representing fire and bombing. This had a large number of varying conditions relating to eligibility but it was basically awarded for three years service in the United Kingdom or one year overseas.

Finally, the War Medal 1939-45 is made of cupro-nickel and has the crowned head of King George VI on the obverse. The reverse shows a lion standing on a defeated dragon, and has the date '1939' above the date '1945'. The ribbon has a narrow red stripe in the centre flanked by two narrow white stripes, thicker dark blue stripes are between the white stripes and the thick red stripes which form the edge of the ribbon. The design represents the Union Flag. The medal was awarded for service of at least twenty-eight days between 3 September 1939 and 2 September 1945.

OTHER CONFLICTS

Specific campaign medals were issued for Korea, 1950-1953, the South Atlantic, 1982, the Gulf, 1990-1991 and Iraq, 2003- . The General Service Medal (1918-1962) was awarded for service in many different campaigns and would always be given with a clasp, sixteen of which were issued. Some examples of these include 'S. Persia' (12 November 1918 - 22 June 1919); 'S.E. Asia 1945-46', awarded to troops serving in the Dutch East Indies and French Indo-China; and 'Cyprus' (1 April 1955 - 18 April 1959). This was succeeded by the Campaign Service Medal in 1962. This was awarded to all three Services, and is often referred to as the General Service Medal.

The Accumulated Campaign Service Medal was introduced in 1994, for 36 months (not necessarily consecutive) operational service. There was also an India General Service Medal, covering campaigns between 1908 to 1935, and 1936 to 1939 and an Africa General Service Medal covering the years 1902 to 1956. The United Nations also issues campaign medals, usually with different ribbons denoting different peace-keeping operations.

LONG SERVICE MEDALS

The Long Service and Good Conduct Medal is self-explanatory. It was initially awarded for twenty-one years service in the infantry or twenty-four years service in the cavalry, but in 1870 this was reduced to eighteen years. **The National Archives** has medal rolls for this award covering the years 1831-1953 in *WO 102*.

The National Archives has awards for the Meritorious Service Medal for the years between 1846 and 1919 in *WO 101*. This was awarded for good service, usually to warrant officers and senior non-commissioned officers, and carried an annuity with it. Between 1916 and 1928 a second type of Meritorious Service Medal was introduced which was an immediate award for single acts of gallantry.

Other similar medals include the Territorial Force Efficiency Medal, the Efficiency Decoration and the Army Emergency Reserve Decoration. Spink and Son have produced many publications relating to these awards.

GALLANTRY AWARDS

Gallantry medals reward a particular action of bravery, but the amount of information available about different decorations does vary considerably. An award can be made more than once, and if this happens the recipient will be given a 'bar' to wear on the original medal's ribbon. Notification of an award (which just gives the information that an individual has been awarded a particular decoration) would be published in the *London Gazette*, a regular publication produced by the Government. Sometimes the citation (a short description of why the award was given) would accompany this, sometimes this would appear in a later issue and sometimes no citation would appear. No citations were published for awards announced in either of the two half-yearly *Honours Lists* published in January (new year) and June (birthday). Few citations were published during the Second World War. There is often a considerable delay between the date of the award and the date that the notification, and the citation if appropriate, was published. Often an individual would be recommended for a particular award, but this would not be granted, or he or she would be awarded a lesser decoration.

The Victoria Cross is the highest gallantry decoration, and is extremely well documented. It can be awarded to all ranks of the three Armed Services. The Department of Documents at the **Imperial War Museum** has a collection of Victoria Cross files which can be consulted by appointment. Anybody interested in this award or the George Cross, which was also awarded to many servicemen, often in connection with bomb disposal, should make an effort to visit the Museum's Victoria Cross and George Cross Gallery. The Museum's web-site also

features the Victoria Cross and the George Cross at these addresses:
Victoria Cross
http://collections.iwm.org.uk/server/show/ConWebDoc.941
George Cross
http://collections.iwm.org.uk/server/show/ConWebDoc.940

The second highest level of gallantry decoration is the Distinguished Service Order for officers, which was introduced in 1886 and the Distinguished Conduct Medal for other ranks, which dates from 1854. These two decorations were replaced by the Conspicuous Gallantry Cross for all ranks in 1993, although the Distinguished Service Order can still be awarded for command and leadership qualities during operations and is now open to all ranks.

Two new gallantry medals were introduced in the First World War. The Military Cross, in December 1914, which could be awarded to junior officers (captains and below) and warrant officers. The Military Medal was instituted in March 1916 for non-commissioned officers and men – women were also eligible. In 1993 awards of the Military Medal were discontinued and the Military Cross became open to all ranks.

Mentions in Despatches were initially introduced for officers only, but by the end of the Boer War both officers and men could be Mentioned in Despatches. It has been estimated that during the First World War 2.3% of army manpower was awarded a Mention in Despatches. No medal was issued but a certificate would be received and in 1920 a multiple-leaved bronze oakleaf emblem was authorised to be worn on the ribbon of the Victory Medal. After 1920 the emblem changed to a single oakleaf, and those awarded in the Second World War were worn on the War Medal 1939-45. Since 1945 those awarded a Mention in Despatches wear the oakleaf emblem on the ribbon of the relevant campaign medal. If the recipient has no campaign medal the emblem can be worn on a piece of khaki cloth shaped as a medal ribbon.

In 1939 the King's (later Queen's) Commendation for Brave Conduct was introduced. This was designed to be a 'civilian' counterpart to a Mention in Despatches, but it was awarded to some soldiers.

During the First and Second World Wars different corps and divisions would often issue gallantry certificates, sometimes accompanied by a badge of honour, but these were never official decorations, although they did confer some local recognition of a heroic deed.

Army personnel (warrant officers and above) have also been appointed to membership of the various Orders of Chivalry, the most notable being the Most Honourable Order of the Bath, Most Distinguished Order of St Michael and St George and the Most Excellent Order of the British Empire. For a very short period in the 1960s and early 1970s the Order of the British Empire was awarded with silver oakleaves for gallantry.

'Permission to accept and wear' foreign orders and decorations would usually be published in the London Gazette, but very little other information exists.

All pre-First World War and First World War gallantry award records have been transferred to **The National Archives** where they can be consulted on microfilm. The National Archives also holds a set of the *London Gazette*, together with the all-important indexes. The **Guildhall Library, Aldermanbury, London EC2P 2EJ**, also holds a complete set with indexes, and acts as the unofficial photocopying service for the *London Gazette* office. The set held by the Imperial War Museum is not quite complete and lacks indexes. It is quite likely that sets of the *London Gazette* will be held by large public reference libraries in various parts of the country.

You can also access the *London Gazette* online at **www.gazettes-online.co.uk**

There is no shortage of published material relating to the Victoria Cross, but The National Archives holds a register of Victoria Cross awards between 1856 and 1957 in *WO 98*. Recipients of the Victoria Cross between 1856 and 1946 can be found in *CAB 106/320*. Citations for Second World War Victoria Crosses are in *CAB 106/312*.

For the Distinguished Service Order and Military Cross in the First World War, The National Archives has a set of record books in *WO 389/1-8*. These consist of pasted extracts from pre-publication copies (containing information later removed for security reasons) of the announcement of awards in the *London Gazette*. They can also contain handwritten annotations. Volumes 2 and 3 of *The VC and DSO* edited by Creagh and Humphris can also be useful. *WO 389/9-24* contains an index for the Military Cross between 1914 and 1938.

The National Archives has indexes for the Distinguished Conduct Medal, the Meritorious Service Medal, the Military

Medal and Mentions in Despatches in the First World War. Some Distinguished Conduct Medal citations were published in the *London Gazette*, and the three published listings by Walker, Brown and McDermott will prove helpful with this. No citations were published for the Meritorious Service Medal, the Military Medal (there were a few exceptions to this – basically those Military Medals awarded to women) and Mentions in Despatches. No citations exist for these First World War awards. The best chance of finding out about the action for which these were awarded is in the unpublished official unit war diary held at The National Archives or in a published unit history or regimental journal (see under the section relating to Regimental Histories). It is also possible that the action may be mentioned in a letter, diary or other personal papers which are now lodged in an archive or museum (the Department of Documents has an extensive collection of such personal papers). It is also always worth checking to see whether records, publications or newspapers which may describe the incident might exist in the soldier's home area. The local studies collection of the relevant library service should be able to advise further about this.

Recommendations for gallantry awards as well as awards for meritorious service between 1935 and 1990 can be found at The National Archives in *WO 373*.

The place to write to for medal claims or medal replacements, although these will only be allowed under extremely stringent conditions, is the **Ministry of Defence Medal Office, Building 250, RAF Innsworth, Gloucester GL3 1HW**. It will be necessary to provide official documentary proof of entitlement.

CASUALTY RECORDS

OFFICIAL RECORDS

More information is likely to be found about an individual if he died in service. Those who died during the two world wars are recorded by the **Commonwealth War Graves Commission, 2 Marlow Road, Maidenhead, Berkshire SL6 7DX**, the organisation which maintains war cemeteries and memorials. This organisation was established in May 1917 as the Imperial War Graves Commission (it changed its name to Commonwealth War Graves Commission in 1960). It had grown out of the Graves Registration Commission, headed by Sir Fabian Ware which had become part of the Army after having originally been under the auspices of the British Red Cross Society. It was decided that bodies would not be allowed to go home for burial but all servicemen and women would be treated equally, being buried where they died and having uniform headstones which would be cared for in perpetuity. Those who did not have a known grave (it was possible that men may have originally been buried but that the markers for these could sometimes be lost or land might be so severely fought over that no identifying features remained) would have their name carved on a memorial. Bodies are still being found on former battlefields and the Commonwealth War Graves Commission is sometimes in the news because of this.

As well as having information about his place of burial or commemoration, they have details of when a soldier died and the unit that he was serving with at the time of his death. Sometimes additional information is included, and because the

Imperial War Graves Commission attempted to send the next of kin a final verification form, often you will find the wife or parents of the soldier listed, together with a home address. The Commonwealth War Graves Commission uses the dates 4 August 1914 - 31 August 1921 and 3 September 1939 - 31 December 1947 for First and Second World War casualties respectively.

The Commonwealth War Graves Commission may charge a small fee for postal enquiries, but information is now computerised and can be accessed on their web-site at **www.cwgc.org** It is not possible to visit the Commonwealth War Graves Commission in person, although they can be contacted by post, telephone or internet. The **Imperial War Museum** has a complete set of Commonwealth War Graves Commission registers in the Reading Room, and these can be worth consulting because as well as a plan of the cemetery, and a map showing the location, they do also give a potted history of the cemetery. This might provide details of hospitals or casualty clearing stations in the area which can be useful if an individual died of wounds. The First World War cemetery registers are more helpful for this as the Second World War cemeteries are larger and more concentrated.

The Department of Printed Books also holds various published histories relating to the Commonwealth War Graves Commission's history and activities.

Details about the burial places of soldiers who died outside the dates covered by the Commonwealth War Graves Commission are held by the **Armed Forces Personnel Administration Agency (JPAC), Joint Casualty and Compassionate**

Centre, Building 182, RAF Innsworth, Gloucester GL3 1HW. Details about soldiers' wives or children who have died outside the United Kingdom should also be held here.

If a non world war casualty died abroad, in what may be termed the South Asia area (covering India, Hong Kong, China, Malaya, Singapore or Dutch East Indies) you may be able to glean some information through the organisation **British Association for Cemeteries in South Asia, 76½ Chartfield Avenue, London SW15 6HQ**. Their listings of cemeteries and memorial inscriptions are held at the **British Library (Asia, Pacific and Africa Collections), 96 Euston Road, London NW1 2DB**. Twice a year, the Association produces the journal *Chowkidar*.

Death certificates for some soldiers who died in hospitals or outside the immediate war zone in France and Belgium between 1914 and 1920 can be found at the **The National Archives** in *RG 35/45-69*.

Death certificates of soldiers who died on active service are held by the Office for National Statistics. A postal service is operated by the **General Register Office, PO Box 2, Southport, Merseyside PR8 2JD**. Indexes can be consulted at the **Family Records Centre, 1 Myddelton Street, London EC1R 1UW**, where certificates can also be purchased in person. There are also separate General Register Offices for Scotland, Northern Ireland and Eire (addresses can be found in Appendix IV). An excellent starting point for more information about death certificates and registration generally is **www.familyrecords.gov.uk**

The **National Army Museum** does have a record of deceased soldiers' effects from 1901-1960, but the First World War records are not yet openly available. These cover the disposal of money owing to soldiers who died whilst serving in the Army. Typically, they will include such details as name, rank, regiment, number, date and place of death, the money owing and who received it. These are not held on site, although National Army Museum staff will search these for a fee and there is a variable turnaround time for this.

PUBLISHED SOURCES

Reference sources held by the Department of Printed Books include the eighty part *Soldiers Died in the Great War, 1914-19* originally published in 1921 by HMSO, and republished by JB Hayward in the late 1980s. A CD-ROM of this is available from Naval and Military Press, and it is quite likely that large public reference libraries will have copies. It is also available online on a pay per view basis at **www.military-genealogy.com**
Access to this can be made through the family history pages of the Imperial War Museum web-site at **www.iwm.org.uk**

Other ranks are listed alphabetically by the battalion of their regiment. Details usually include full name, place of birth, place of enlistment and sometimes place of residence, regimental number, rank, the cause of death (killed in action, died of wounds, or died, for death by natural causes such as disease, drowning, etc), theatre of death and date of death. The cause of death may provide some additional clues for research – those who were killed in action may have been involved in a big attack or might have been hit by a stray shell or bullet; often there will be no known grave and the soldier will be commemorated on one of the **Commonwealth War Graves Commission**'s memorials. Those who died of wounds are likely to have received some medical treatment, and by double-checking what the unit was doing on the day of death or a few days before it and how close to the front line the cemetery is, you may be able to make an educated guess at when he was wounded. Those who died of natural causes will usually have a grave (unless they drowned or were on a ship that sank), and this may well be in the vicinity of one of the large base hospitals. *Soldiers Died in the Great War* will also include gallantry medals if these were awarded and details of the former regiment together with the former regimental number if applicable. A sample entry reads:

> Martin, Alfred Edgar, b.[orn] Highbury, e.[nlisted] London ([place of residence] E. Finchley), 763536, L/Cpl., k.[illed] in a.[ction], F.[rance] & F.[landers], 30/12/17.

Because of the enormous numbers listed in these publications it was inevitable that some mistakes would be made, and as long as this can be supplemented by documentary evidence, we make every effort to annotate and correct the copies that we hold.

There is a single volume of *Officers Died in the Great War, 1914-1919*, but this is less detailed. A sample entry reads:

> Salisbury, Cecil Roland, 2/Lt. (Tp.[Temporary]), k. in a., 7/5/17.

It has probably been superseded by *Cross of Sacrifice: Volume I: Officers who Died in the Service of British, Indian and East African Regiments and Corps, 1914-1919* by SD and DB Jarvis, which gives a listing in alphabetical order, so it is not essential to know the regiment. It also provides details of the Commonwealth War Graves Commission cemetery or memorial register in which the officer's name can be found – and this can be easily checked in the **Imperial War Museum**'s Reading Room.

Many rolls of honour were published during and after the First World War, and the Imperial War Museum does have an excellent collection of these. Some began to be compiled at the start of the war and presumably were unable to cope with the unprecedented number of casualties. One excellent source is de Ruvigny's *Roll of Honour*, which is unusual in that it features both officers and other ranks, and many of the entries include a small photograph. We have the first two volumes of this (worth checking if a soldier died in 1914 or 1915) and the fifth. The **British Library** has all five volumes.

There are some publications which list those who died in particular events, such as the first day of the Somme, or officers who died at Gallipoli.

Some rolls of honour include details about those who survived as well as those who died. The Department of Printed Books has a large number of rolls compiled by schools, universities, localities, societies, railways, churches and commercial organisations. We also have a good collection of local town histories, which can sometimes list names.

A frequently requested although notoriously unreliable publication is *The National Roll of the Great War, 1914-1918.* This is unusual in that it lists both those who died and those who survived, as well as those involved in non-military war work, such as female munitions workers. However, we believe it to have been compiled on a subscription basis, and as such, is very far from being comprehensive. It also covers only a few geographical areas, such as large towns and cities. The publication is believed to have begun in 1920, but by 1922 the publishers had gone into liquidation, having published only fourteen volumes, referred to as sections. The sections published were: 1.London 2.London 3.London 4.Southampton 5.Luton 6.Birmingham 7.London 8.Leeds 9.Bradford 10.Portsmouth 11. Manchester 12.Bedford and Northampton 13.London 14.Salford. All fourteen sections are held by the Imperial War Museum, as well as an index volume recently published by Naval and Military Press. The Manchester and Salford volumes can be viewed online on the *Spinning the Web: the Story of the Cotton Industry* web-site at **www.spinningtheweb.org.uk**

There are commercially produced rolls of honour for the Second World War, although nowhere near as many as for the Great War.

It is always worth investigating these sources, as even if they are not held by the Department of Printed Books there might be useful listings, local histories or contemporary local newspapers held in the home area of the soldier you are researching. Schools, churches, clubs and commercial organisations may have published magazines featuring letters from those on active service and keeping their readers up to date with the activities and whereabouts of their friends and colleagues. This is a source of information that is often neglected, possibly because it does involve very time-consuming research. The **British Library Newspaper Library, Colindale Avenue, London NW9 5HE**, has copies of newspapers from all over the country.

The recent increase in interest in family history and the world wars has led to many new publications about war memorials and the local citizens who served. The Department of Printed Books actively seeks to acquire this type of material and we are always grateful to have works of this nature brought to our attention. Local studies libraries and county record offices should be able to advise further on the type of material which might be available.

The Museum has a computer coded roll of honour for the Second World War which was compiled by the War Office. It is difficult and unwieldy to use, and it is necessary to know the regiment that an individual served with. This is also held at **The National Archives** in *WO 304* and is now available on CD-ROM produced by Naval and Military Press. This can be seen in the Imperial War Museum's Reading Room. It can also be consulted on a pay per view basis on the web-site **www.military-genealogy.com**

The Department of Printed Books also holds published rolls of honour for other conflicts such as Korea and Malaya.

Regimental histories often contain rolls of honour, and some especially detailed unit histories may include details of how individuals died. Regimental journals sometimes include informative rolls of honour, for example, the *Journal of the Royal*

Scots Fusiliers, Volume XIII, Number 2, dated October 1945, has a quite detailed regimental roll of honour for the Second World War.

UNITED KINGDOM NATIONAL INVENTORY OF WAR MEMORIALS

Some rolls of honour can be found on leaflets or programmes relating to the building and unveiling of war memorials. The Imperial War Museum launched an appeal shortly after the end of the First World War for this type of information and the Department of Printed Books has a large ephemera collection relating to war memorials, whilst the Photograph Archive has photographs. The **United Kingdom National Inventory of War Memorials (UKNIWM)** based at the Imperial War Museum is compiling a listing of all war memorials in the United Kingdom. You can conduct a search at the website **www.ukniwm.org.uk**

The initial aim of the project was to record the memorials, but in some cases, the names and additional material were sent to the UKNIWM. The names have now been input onto a searchable 'virtual memorial' that can be added to by members of the public, in conjunction with Channel 4. You can find this database at **www.channel4.com/history/microsites/L/lostgeneration/index.html**

The UKNIWM is always interested to learn of any memorial that might not have already been recorded. Contact details are **United Kingdom National Inventory of War Memorials, Imperial War Museum, Lambeth Road, London SE1 6HZ**.

MEDICAL RECORDS

Very few medical records have survived from the First World War – most of them were destroyed in 1975. Sample records are held in class *MH 106* at **The National Archives**, and include most records for the Grenadier Guards, the Leicestershire Regiment and Hussars, and a few for the Royal Field Artillery and Royal Flying Corps. A few admission books are available for some medical facilities. There are war diaries for Hospitals, Field Ambulances and Casualty Clearing Stations, but these are unlikely to have details relating to individuals.

If you are interested in reading about what happened when a soldier was wounded, the various official history volumes prove extremely helpful. These explain the various chains of evacuations as well as providing information about hospital provision, administration, pathology, etc.

The Department of Printed Books holds a good selection of books relating to all aspects of health and medicine in both world wars.

The Department of Printed Books also holds a set of *War Office Weekly Casualty Lists* from December 1917 to February 1919 which contain references to killed, wounded and captured servicemen. This is a difficult and unrewarding source to use. No specific dates are given other than the general issue date of the *List*, and entries have been proven to appear several months after the occasion to which they refer.

Throughout the First World War the Enquiry for the Wounded and Missing Department of the British Red Cross and Order of St John issued monthly *Enquiry Lists* with fortnightly supplements. These were listings of wounded and missing soldiers, compiled from official and unofficial sources, for use by searchers in the United Kingdom and abroad. Individual entries are listed by regiment, and contain details of battalion, occasionally of company and platoon, and date. Of the fifty volumes produced between 1915-1919, only a few have survived, and the Department of Printed Books holds the following issues:

> [February 1915]; 18 May 1915; 26 June 1915; 17 July 1915, supplement B; 24 July 1915, supplement B; 31 July 1915, supplement B; 7 August 1915, supplement B; 14 August 1915, supplement B; 4 September 1915; 18 September 1915, supplement no. 2; 1 February 1916; 15 September 1916, supplement [photocopy]; 1 August 1917, no. 14 [1989 reprint by Sunset Militaria and Ray Westlake]; 1 October 1918, no. 17; 1 December 1918, no. 21.

The National Archives holds some pension records in the papers of the Paymaster General's Office (PRO class *PMG*). This office was responsible for service pay and pensions until 1916 when the Ministry of Pensions was founded and the responsibility was shared. It should be noted that class *PMG* usually relates only to officers. Various ledgers relating to the First World War period and disability retired pay, supplementary allowances and special grants, pensions to relatives of deceased officers, widows' pensions, children's allowances and pay to relatives of missing officers can be found in classes *PMG 42-47*. A selection of papers from the Ministry of Pensions can also be found at The National Archives in *PIN*

26 and *PIN 82*. The former class contains a cross-section of disability and widows' pension files, and consists of over 20,000 files. About one in twelve claims for widows' and dependents' pensions survives in class *PIN 82*. Each form would contain details of the soldier's name and home address, some details of his service, the date and place of injury and death, and information about the pension awarded.

ADDITIONAL SOURCES

REGIMENTAL AND CAMPAIGN HISTORIES

Once you know the unit your relative served with you can begin to find out more about it and where it would have served. There are a variety of sources that can help you with this.

ORDERS OF BATTLE

You will be able to work out how your relative's unit fitted into the military forces in a particular campaign by using the Orders of Battle.

There are various published sources which can help you to find out about the higher formations that units served with. Cavalry and infantry regiments are the easiest to trace and James's *British Regiments, 1914-1918* will prove invaluable for this. It gives a brief history of every battalion in an infantry regiment and every cavalry regiment, including when it was raised or where it was when the First World War broke out. It also contains details of the brigade and division the battalion was attached to (including details of when this might have changed), as well as the dates that it arrived in a particular theatre of war. It also tells you where the unit was on 11 November 1918, or when it had disbanded or amalgamated if this happened earlier. This information is now readily available on *The Long, Long Trail* web-site at **www.1914-1918.net** – and it also provides the brigade and divisional information described in the paragraph below.

There are also a number of published orders of battle, which provide details of various army formations and show where the different units served. Becke's multi-volume *Order of Battle of Divisions* is especially useful for giving a potted history of the division as well as showing the composition at various stages during the war, as it was quite common for units to move around. There is no index to this so it is helpful if you already know the division you are looking for. This can be checked either in James, or in the War Office issued *Order of Battle of British Armies in France (including Lines of Communication Units)...*, which we have for September 1917, November 1917, February 1918, March 1918 and November 1918. The official history volumes and some campaign histories will also have orders of battle at the back.

For the Second World War, Joslen's two volume *Orders of Battle* are helpful, although nowhere near as detailed as their First World War equivalent. Another useful publication, which rearranges much of the information in Joslen as well as giving some additional material is *British Army Orders of Battle, 1939-1945: a Finding List – Supplement to Joslen* by Butler and Lockerby.

The constantly evolving web-site *Land Forces of Britain, the Empire and Commonwealth* promises to be helpful for working out the different commands and higher formations that units served under. The address is **www.regiments.org**

UNIT WAR DIARIES
The unpublished official unit war diary should be held at **The National Archives**. From 1907 all units on active service were obliged to maintain a unit war diary, sometimes known as

intelligence summaries. This was a daily report about events that had happened in the unit and any actions they had been involved with. The level of information did vary from unit to unit but usually they do not mention individuals, (except officers). Sometimes these can be quite difficult to read owing to poor handwriting (especially if they were being written under stressful circumstances), pencil fading or the fact that they are not good quality carbon copies. The National Archives also has copies of the trench maps that the war diaries were intended to be used in conjunction with (*WO 153*). First World War war diaries from 1914 to 1922 are held at The National Archives in *WO 95* and are arranged by theatre of operations, then by army, corps and division. Some diaries (containing confidential information) were restricted (*WO 154*) but are now open.

The National Archives have begun to put First World War war diaries on the Documents Online section of their web-site, where they can be viewed for a fee. The web-site address is **www.nationalarchives.gov.uk/documentsonline**

Second World War war diaries are now open and again they are arranged according to the theatre in which the unit fought. Different commands have different reference numbers, and you can find more information about these through The National Archives web-site.

War diaries were also kept when units were on active service outside the period of the two world wars, for example, war diaries from units in Shanghai between 1927-1932 can be found in *WO 191*, or units in Korea between 1950-1953 can be found in *WO 281*.

Between 1946 and 1950 Quarterly Historical Reports were maintained, although these were less detailed than war diaries. In 1950 these were replaced by the Unit Historical Record. These can be seen in *WO 305*, although they are subject to the 30 year closure rule.

PUBLISHED HISTORIES

The war diary would form the basis for the published regimental or battalion history but this would also draw on other sources, and will probably be more detailed than the unit war diary. The Department of Printed Books has an excellent collection of these, including some which are not mentioned in White's *Bibliography of Regimental Histories of the British Army*. These often contain rolls of honour, listings of gallantry awards, maps, etc. Some regiments, such as the Northumberland Fusiliers, do not have a general regimental history for the First World War, but several individual battalion histories were published. Often a regimental history will cover many different battalions and consequently may not be very detailed. Although officers are often mentioned, you are unlikely to find individual soldiers mentioned by name.

Few infantry brigade histories were published, but there were a large number of divisional histories and these will provide additional information. If you are really unfortunate and there are no published histories for the battalion, regiment, brigade or division, you can check to see which higher formations the unit you are interested in was brigaded with, and consult those histories.

When you know the unit that an individual served with, you will be able to work out the higher formations that he served with and therefore use the multi-volume official history sets. These were published several years after the various campaigns, but provide detailed accounts of what was happening in particular theatres between various dates. The Imperial War Museum has republished the various First World War official history volumes, and these can be purchased directly from us. Some Second World War volumes have also been republished. These can be purchased through Naval and Military Press at **www.naval-military-press.com**

The Department of Printed Books has produced a large number of booklists relating to different campaigns, and most of these are available through the Museum's web-site. These contain the titles of several books that you can make an appointment to consult in the Reading Room, or which may be available through the inter-library loan scheme.

MAPS
The Department of Printed Books also has an excellent map collection, especially for the Western Front in the First World War. It is possible to get black and white copies of maps but you do need to be quite specific in your request. Maps from the First World War can also be found at The National Archives. Peter Chasseaud's books about trench maps will prove helpful for anybody trying to find out more about these.

PERSONAL ACCOUNTS
Autobiographies should not be overlooked as these will provide information about what it felt like to be at the Battle of the Somme, or at El Alamein, or part of the British Army of the Rhine. These give details at the human level and will enable you to have an insight into what the individual might have experienced. The Department of Printed Books has a

large collection of published biographies and autobiographies. The Department of Documents and the Sound Archive also have similar material consisting of letters, diaries or unpublished manuscripts, and oral interview recordings respectively. All of these can be accessed simply by booking an appointment with the appropriate department. There are also other institutions such as regimental museums and universities that might hold personal papers.

BATTLEFIELD GUIDES

Often when researching the military service of a family member, there will be a desire to retrace his footsteps, which may mean visiting a grave or memorial or seeing where actions would have been fought. The Department of Printed Books has a good collection of battlefield guides ranging from the Somme to Gallipoli and Normandy to Hong Kong, and these can help with planning trips abroad. Many of the more recent publications will be available through other libraries but we also have First World War battlefield guides dating from the early 1920s.

REGIMENTAL MAGAZINES AND NEWSPAPERS

Regimental journals are an under-used source, and the Department of Printed Books does have a good collection of these, although it does tend to be stronger for the Second World War period onwards. We do have an excellent, although unpublished, four volume work by Lake listing the various regimental magazines and where they can be found. Our collection ranges from trench journals to divisional newsletters and regimental periodicals to regular publications issued by particular commands. Sometimes these can be helpful for movements of officers and men during combat – for example the *St George's Gazette*, the regimental journal of the Northumberland Fusiliers which we have from 1914, sometimes provides details of movements of officers, promotions and men taken prisoner.

The magazine *Soldier*, which began life in 1944 and still continues today, is a mine of information, and would be well worth consulting by anyone interested in finding out about the general life of a soldier in the latter part of the Second World War or the National Serviceman.

Journals are especially useful for finding out about Regular soldiers during peacetime and they can prove helpful for tracing details about wives and children of soldiers. Sometimes the date that a soldier joins a regiment will be mentioned, and they will often be welcomed or bade farewell in various reports. There are usually columns for births, marriages (more modern issues sometimes carry wedding photographs), and deaths – sometimes detailed obituaries are included. Sporting fixtures and events such as amateur dramatics tend to be given wide coverage, so if your ancestor enjoyed these types of activities there is a good chance that he may be mentioned. Photographs and detailed accounts of activities in a particular station will provide enormous insight into exactly what a soldier would have been doing while stationed in India, Hong Kong or Aldershot.

REGIMENTAL MUSEUMS

Regimental museums can be useful sources of information although the amount and content of the material held will vary. They do not usually hold service records as these are held centrally, and you should try to find as much information as you can from The National Archives, Army Personnel Centre or local sources before contacting the regimantal museum. Most will have a comprehensive collection of regimental histories, journals, personal papers and artefacts, as well as extremely knowledgeable curators, and these may be more convenient to visit, by appointment, for those who live far from London. Please bear in mind that regimental museums are likely to suffer from understaffing and underfunding, and will be unable to do research for you. The publication *A Guide to Military Museums and other Places of Military Interest* by Terence and Shirley Wise will prove helpful for contact details, as will the *Army Museums Ogilby Trust* web-site at **www.armymuseums.org.uk**

Regimental and Old Comrades Associations can also be helpful, and it may be possible to contact individuals who may have known the soldier you are tracing. These can be especially helpful with those regiments which have no museum or which had only a short existence. Some of these addresses are given in Appendix IV. There are also some web-sites which might be of assistance, although many of these are 'unofficial' sites.

You can write to journals and association newsletters in an attempt to contact people who may remember the person you are tracing or who may be conducting research similar to your own. Contemporary regimental journals can prove helpful – the Department of Printed Books can advise about relevant addresses.

There are also some organisations dedicated to studying various campaigns and sharing research interests. For example, the **Western Front Association** is a large organisation with many local groups covering a wider area of interest than its title might suggest. *Stand To!*, a journal containing useful and pertinent articles is published three times a year, as is *Bulletin*, a newsletter.

Some useful web-site addresses for First World War campaigns are:
Western Front Association: **www.westernfront.co.uk**
Gallipoli Association: **www.gallipoli-association.org**
Salonika Campaign Society: **www.salonika.freeserve.co.uk**

GENEALOGICAL SOURCES

MAGAZINES
Family history has become extremely popular in recent years and there are many magazines on the market which offer advice and guidance. The Imperial War Museum has subscribed to *Family Tree Magazine* since 1989, (back copies can be consulted in our Reading Room), but there have been many new publications of this sort produced in recent years. *Family Tree Magazine* is published monthly by **ABM Publishing, 61 Great Whyte, Ramsey, Huntingdon, Cambridgeshire PE26 1HJ**. Other titles include *Family History News and Digest* produced by the Federation of Family History Societies, *Genealogists Magazine* by the Society of Genealogists, *Ancestors* published by The National Archives and *Family History Monthly*. Contact details for all these can be found in Appendix IV.

SOCIETIES
Genealogical societies, such as the **Federation of Family History Societies, c/o FFHS Administrator, PO Box 2425, Coventry CV5 6YX** and the **Society of**

Genealogists, 14 Charterhouse Buildings, Goswell Road, London EC1M 7BA, may be able to offer advice, as well as provide details of local societies and organisations. There are all sorts of societies concentrating on local areas, individual names, occupations, nationalities, etc. Both the Federation of Family History Societies and the Society of Genealogists have also produced useful guides for the family historian, some of which are listed in Appendix V.

LOCAL LIBRARIES AND ARCHIVES

Information held in your relative's home area should not be overlooked. Sources such as local histories, rolls of honour and newspapers, described in the Casualty Records section, can be excellent sources. One other often overlooked but potentially helpful resource is the Absent Voters List, detailed below.

The Family and Local History Handbook, published annually, is full of genealogical and historical articles of interest to the beginner and experienced researcher alike. It also contains contact details for a wide variety of registrars of births, marriages and deaths, record offices, libraries, museums and societies.

An online listing of record repositories can be found at **www.nationalarchives.gov.uk/archon**
The National Register of Archives – available online at **www.nationalarchives.gov.uk/nra** – will allow some searching of archival catalogues. Details about family and local history resources located in public libraries, together with contact details, can be found at **www.familia.org.uk**

ABSENT VOTERS LISTS

Some basic information should also be found in either the Absent Voters Lists of 1918 or the Service Voters Registers of 1945, although this does assume that the soldier was alive or in service at the date they were compiled. These were produced in order to enable servicemen, over the age of 21, to vote in the constituency of their home address, and should be located in the local studies collection of the relevant library service or county record office.

A few Absent Voters Lists from the First World War can now be found on the internet. To find out what is held in the area your relative came from, and how to gain access to it, you can check on the web-site **www.familia.org.uk**

Online Absent Voters Lists:

Accrington: **www.pals.org.uk/avl/index.htm**

Grimsby and Cleethorpes:
www.angelfire.com/de/delighted/voters.html

Leeds: **www.leeds.gov.uk** [search under Online Databases]

Wakefield:
www.wakefieldfhs.org.uk/abscent%20voters.htm

THE INTERNET

The internet has revolutionised family history research, and there are many web-sites that can help you, either by giving advice, helping with a specific subject, or allowing you to contact individuals or appeal for information. Not everything that appears on the internet is current or correct information, and you should always check to see who has created the web-site and what their aim is. Some web-site addresses appear in Appendix IV, but you should be aware that web-sites sometimes just disappear, and that new ones are springing into life all the time. Following links from one site to another can often be a rewarding activity, if sometimes frustrating.

An excellent site for those starting out is **www.familyrecords.gov.uk** as this explains what records you can expect to find and how to locate them, as well as providing links. Other sites that might be helpful are Cyndi's List at **www.cyndislist.com** and GENUKI at **www.genuki.org.uk**

For tracing ex-servicemen and women, there are a number of web-sites that you can contact. The Royal British Legion web-site at **www.britishlegion.org.uk** features a 'Lost Trails' section. A couple of other sites are MOD Reunited at **www.modreunited.com** and Forces Reunited at **www.forcesreunited.org.uk**

FAMILY HISTORY FAIRS

Family History fairs are held regularly around the country, and can be excellent places for both beginners and experienced researchers to find out what is available. The Imperial War Museum does sometimes participate in larger fairs, and also regularly has family history days in the Museum galleries. Visitors are welcome to come and ask questions, and staff are able to spend longer dealing with these than we are normally able to do in the course of our work. The Museum web-site family history pages has details of the dates of these events.

MILITARY WIVES AND CHILDREN

Regular soldiers who made a career of the Army would often get married and have families, which would move around with them according to their postings. Records of births, marriages and deaths are held by the **Office for National Statistics**, and these can be checked in the indexes at the **Family Records Centre**. **The National Archives** is a good source for pre-1914 information and does have some registers of births held in *WO 156* which cover part of the twentieth century. These are registers of births at Shorncliffe and Hythe, 1878-1939; Dover Castle, 1865-1916 and 1929-1940; Buttervant, 1917-1922; and Fermoy, 1920-1921. *WO 256* includes baptisms and banns of marriage for army personnel in Palestine between 1939 and 1947.

Army children usually had decent education at least to an elementary level and the book *Tommy Atkins' Children* will provide more information about this. The Duke of York's Royal Military School, now located in Dover, and the Royal Hibernian Military School in Dublin, which amalgamated with the former in 1924, were both established in order to take children of soldiers who had been orphaned or lost a parent. Admission and discharge registers for the Duke of York's Royal Military School between 1803-1923 can be found at The National Archives in *WO 143/17-25*. *WO 143/70* contains a record of admissions to the school between 1906-1956. Few records still exist for the Royal Hibernian School but an index of admissions which contains annotations to about 1919 can be found in *WO 143/27*.

Regimental journals can be a good source of information about life for military families, and sometimes feature a 'wives page'. This is especially the case in the post-1945 period when living conditions and expectations improved, and today a regular magazine *Army Families Journal: the Voice of the Families* is published. If you are interested in reading more about this, the books *On the Strength* and *Judy O'Grady and the Colonel's Lady* will prove of interest.

APPENDIX I

REGIMENTAL AND ARMY NUMBERS

The whole issue of regimental and army numbers is a complex one. Before and during the First World War soldiers had been issued with regimental numbers which changed every time a soldier changed his unit and so it was quite common for a soldier to have had more than one number throughout his period of service. This did cause problems and a simplified system was introduced in 1920 which gave a man an army number which would stay with him throughout his military service, even if he changed units.

From 1857 officers were issued with Long Numbers, but this number referred to the officer's file rather than the man himself. In 1921 it was decided to provide officers with Personal Numbers and this system began in 1922, although the P/number was still written on and identified the officer's file as soon as this was opened.

Before 1914 the regimental numbering system had been perfectly adequate, but with the enormous increase in men serving in the Army following the outbreak of war the situation rapidly became chaotic. The regimental number would precede the soldier's name in all documentation, and would be retained should he become a warrant officer, although if a soldier was to become a commissioned officer he would no longer use this and would receive a Long Number, or in later years, a Personal Number. Generally speaking each battalion within a regiment would have its own numbering sequence, and numbers would be issued consecutively. The result of this was that several soldiers in a regiment, in different battalions, would have the same regimental number. *King's Regulations* of 1912 (paragraphs 1897-1900 refer to regimental numbers, but the whole section to paragraph 1941 on records and what documentation originally existed, might be of interest to the family historian) expressly stated that numbers were not to be reused, ie if a soldier died, deserted, transferred or was discharged, but there is evidence that this did happen. Blocks of numbers were also issued to Base Camps in France and other overseas areas where they could be given to men who were being rushed to the front line or who might have been wounded and were being allocated to another unit. This could result in a soldier being issued with a new number which was quite different to the one on his identity disc, and this could cause severe problems if the soldier subsequently died.

Army Council Instruction 2414 dated December 1916 gave details about a new numbering system that was to be applied to the Territorial Force, which would give every man a six digit number. This was to come into effect on 1 March 1917 although there were to be some deviations from this. The full listing of these blocks of numbers can be found in the appendix to this *ACI*. The numbers were allocated to the different Territorial battalions (this would include the first and second line battalions, although by this date the third line battalions were in the process of being converted to Training Reserve formations) within the regiment and these were arranged in the *ACI* alphabetically rather than by order of precedence. The blocks of numbers were in fact duplicated, so that the first Territorial battalion of each regiment started off with a 200,000 number. The numbers given to each regiment varied, but the range of numbers for the first listed regiment – the Argyll and Sutherland Highlanders is as follows:

5th Battalion	200,001 - 250,000
6th Battalion	250,001 - 275,000
7th Battalion	275,001 - 300,000
8th Battalion	300,001 - 325,000
9th Battalion	325,001 - 350,000
16th Battalion	350,001 - 375,000

The London Regiment naturally had the highest range of numbers, with the 32nd Battalion being allocated numbers in the range 840,001 - 860,000.

Some regimental numbers featured prefixes, which can provide information – for example the main number might be prefixed with a number such as '3-' or '6/'. This number might relate to the battalion of the regiment that he served in, but could also be carried to a different battalion within the same regiment. Letters could also be used – for example, the Army Service Corps had a variety of letters which were used and these can identify the type of work which the soldier would have been engaged in. The initials 'R' denote a man who served with the Remount Branch and would have worked with horses, 'S' indicates the Supply Branch, 'T' indicates Transport and 'M' indicates Mechanical Transport, ie motorised transport. There were other initials which could be used, such as a second 'S' which would suggest specialised skills.

Many other letters prefix regimental numbers and as little documentary evidence exists to provide a definite explanation for these it is often a case of providing an educated guess. Examples of these include 'GS', which probably stands for General Service, 'G' probably stands for the same, and 'S' for Service. 'TR' probably stands for Training Reserve. If you are interested in finding out more about this you might like to read back issues of, or subscribe to *Orders and Medals: the Journal of the Orders and Medals Research Society*.

You may also conduct your own research or gain a rough idea of when a soldier might have joined a particular battalion by examining ranges of numbers in a particular unit and dates of death in *Soldiers Died in the Great War*. Information can also be found by examining the Medal Roll Registers at The National Archives.

In August 1920 *Army Order* 338 changed the numbering system from a regimental to an army number which would remain with a soldier throughout his military service. The block of numbers is given below – this may prove useful if you are tracing a Second World War soldier and know his number but not his regiment. It is to be noted that many of these units were disbanded shortly after the allocation of the new numbers, such as most of the Irish Regiments, the Machine Gun Corps and the Corps of Military Accountants, and therefore many numbers were never used. The ordering of the blocks of numbers was done according to the location of the various Record Offices. The soldier who was allocated the sought after number 1 was Sergeant Major George James Redman of the Royal Army Service Corps:

Royal Army Service Corps	I - 294,000
Household Cavalry	
1st Life Guards	294,001 - 299,000
2nd Life Guards	299,001 - 304,000
Royal Horse Guards	304,001 - 309,000
Cavalry of the Line	309,001 - 721,000

This was originally broken down by the following categories

Lancers	309,001 - 386,000
Dragoons	386,001 - 528,000
Hussars	528,001 - 721,000

and the numbers 558,471 - 558,761 were later allocated to the Royal Armoured Corps

Royal Artillery	721,001 - 1,842,000

This was originally broken down by the following categories, until 1924

Royal Horse and Royal Field Artillery	721,001 - 1,396,000
Honourable Artillery Company	1,396,001 - 1,400,000
Royal Garrison Artillery	1,400,001 - 1,842,000
Royal Engineers	1,842,001 - 2,303,000
Royal Corps of Signals	2,303,001 - 2,604,000

Originally came under the Royal Engineers – the Royal Corps of Signals was established in 1920

Grenadier Guards	2,604,001 - 2,646,000
Coldstream Guards	2,646,001 - 2,688,000
Scots Guards	2,688,001 - 2,714,000
Irish Guards	2,714,001 - 2,730,000
Welsh Guards	2,730,001 - 2,744,000
Black Watch (Royal Highlanders)	2,744,001 - 2,809,000
Seaforth Highlanders	2,809,001 - 2,865,000
Gordon Highlanders	2,865,001 - 2,921,000
Cameron Highlanders	2,921,001 - 2,966,000
Argyll and Sutherland Highlanders	2,966,001 - 3,044,000

Royal Scots	3,044,001 - 3,122,000
Royal Scots Fusiliers	3,122,001 - 3,178,000
King's Own Scottish Borderers	3,178,001 - 3,233,000
Cameronians (Scottish Rifles)	3,233,001 - 3,299,000
Highland Light Infantry	3,299,001 - 3,377,000
East Lancashire Regiment	3,377,001 - 3,433,000
Lancashire Fusiliers	3,433,001 - 3,511,000
Manchester Regiment	3,511,001 - 3,589,000
Border Regiment	3,589,001 - 3,644,000
South Lancashire Regiment (Prince of Wales's Volunteers)	3,644,001 - 3,701,000
King's Own Royal Regiment (Lancaster)	3,701,001 - 3,757,000
King's Regiment (Liverpool)	3,757,001 - 3,846,000
Loyal Regiment (North Lancashire)	3,846,001 - 3,902,000
South Wales Borderers	3,902,001 - 3,947,000
Welch Regiment	3,947,001 - 4,025,000
King's Shropshire Light Infantry	4,025,001 - 4,070,000
Monmouthshire Regiment	4,070,001 - 4,103,000
Herefordshire Regiment	4,103,001 - 4,114,000
Cheshire Regiment	4,114,001 - 4,178,000
Royal Welch Fusiliers	4,178,001 - 4,256,000
Northumberland Fusiliers	4,256,001 - 4,334,000
East Yorkshire Regiment	4,334,001 - 4,379,000
Green Howards (Alexandra, Princess of Wales's Own Yorkshire Regiment)	4,379,001 - 4,435,000
Durham Light Infantry	4,435,001 - 4,523,000
West Yorkshire Regiment	4,523,001 - 4,601,000
Duke of Wellington's Regiment (West Riding)	4,601,001 - 4,680,000
King's Own Yorkshire Light Infantry	4,680,001 - 4,736,000
York and Lancaster Regiment	4,736,001 - 4,792,000
Lincolnshire Regiment	4,792,001 - 4,848,000

Leicestershire Regiment	4,848,001 - 4,904,000
South Staffordshire Regiment	4,904,001 - 4,960,000
Sherwood Foresters	4,960,001 - 5,038,000
(Nottinghamshire and Derbyshire Regiment)	
North Staffordshire Regiment	5,038,001 - 5,094,000
Royal Warwickshire Regiment	5,094,001 - 5,172,000
Gloucestershire Regiment	5,172,001 - 5,239,000
Worcestershire Regiment	5,239,001 - 5,328,000
Royal Berkshire Regiment	5,328,001 - 5,373,000
Oxfordshire and Buckinghamshire Light Infantry	5,373,001 - 5,429,000
Duke of Cornwall's Light Infantry	5,429,001 - 5,485,000
Hampshire Regiment	5,485,001 - 5,562,000
Wiltshire Regiment	5,562,001 - 5,608,000
Devonshire Regiment	5,608,001 - 5,662,000
Somerset Light Infantry	5,662,001 - 5,718,000
Dorsetshire Regiment	5,718,001 - 5,763,000
Norfolk Regiment	5,763,001 - 5,819,000
Suffolk Regiment	5,819,001 - 5,875,000
Northamptonshire Regiment	5,875,001 - 5,931,000
Cambridgeshire Regiment	5,931,001 - 5,942,000
Bedfordshire and Hertfordshire Regiment	5,942,001 - 5,998,000
Essex Regiment	5,998,001 - 6,076,000
Queen's Royal Regiment (West Surrey)	6,076,001 - 6,132,000
East Surrey Regiment	6,132,001 - 6,188,000
Middlesex Regiment	6,188,001 - 6,278,000
Buffs (East Kent Regiment)	6,278,001 - 6,334,000
Royal West Kent Regiment	6,334,001 - 6,390,000
Royal Sussex Regiment	6,390,001 - 6,446,000
Royal Fusiliers	6,446,001 - 6,515,000
London Regiment	6,515,001 - 6,825,000

In 1933 the London Record and Pay Office closed, and the administration was conducted by the Corps of which the Regiments formed part:

1st City of London Regiment	6,515,001 - 6,526,500
2nd City of London Regiment	6,526,501 - 6,538,000
3rd City of London Regiment	6,538,001 - 6,549,500
4th City of London Regiment	6,549,501 - 6,561,000
5th City of London Regiment	6,561,001 - 6,572,500
6th City of London Regiment	6,572,501 - 6,584,000
7th City of London Regiment	6,584,001 - 6,595,500
8th City of London Regiment	6,595,501 - 6,607,000
9th London Regiment	6,607,001 - 6,618,500
10th London Regiment	6,618,501 - 6,630,000
11th London Regiment	6,630,001 - 6,641,500
12th London Regiment	6,641,501 - 6,653,000
13th London Regiment	6,653,001 - 6,664,500
14th London Regiment	6,664,501 - 6,676,000
15th London Regiment	6,676,001 - 6,687,500
16th London Regiment	6,687,501 - 6,699,000
17th London Regiment	6,699,001 - 6,710,500
18th London Regiment	6,710,501 - 6,722,000
19th London Regiment	6,722,001 - 6,733,500
20th London Regiment	6,733,501 - 6,745,000
21st London Regiment	6,745,001 - 6,756,500
22nd London Regiment	6,756,501 - 6,768,000
23rd London Regiment	6,768,001 - 6,779,500
24th London Regiment	6,779,501 - 6,791,000
25th London Regiment	6,791,001 - 6,802,500
Inns of Court Regiment	6,802,501 - 6,814,000
Inns of Court Officer Training Corps	6,814,001 - 6,825,000
Honourable Artillery Company	6,825,001 - 6,837,000
(Infantry)	

King's Royal Rifle Corps	6,837,001 - 6,905,000
Rifle Brigade	6,905,001 - 6,972,000
Royal Inniskilling Fusiliers	6,972,001 - 7,006,000
Royal Irish Rifles	7,006,001 - 7,040,000

renamed Royal Ulster Rifles in 1921

Royal Irish Fusiliers	7,040,001 - 7,075,000
Royal Dublin Fusiliers disbanded 1922	7,075,001 - 7,109,000
Royal Irish Regiment	7,109,001 - 7,143,000
Connaught Rangers disbanded 1922	7,143,001 - 7,177,000
Leinster Regiment disbanded 1922	7,177,001 - 7,211,000
Royal Munster Fusiliers disbanded 1922	7,211,001 - 7,245,000
Royal Army Medical Corps	7,245,001 - 7,539,000

the numbers between 7,536,001 - 7,539,000 were later allocated to the Army Dental Corps

Channel Islands Militia	7,539,001 - 7,574,000

consisted of the Royal Guernsey Militia, Royal Alderney Artillery Militia and Royal Militia of the Island of Jersey – discontinued in 1929

Royal Army Ordnance Corps	7,574,001 - 7,657,000
Royal Army Pay Corps	7,657,001 - 7,681,000
Corps of Military Police	7,681,001 - 7,717,000
Military Provost Staff Corps	7,717,001 - 7,718,800
Small Arms School	7,718,801 - 7,720,400
Army Educational Corps	7,720,401 - 7,732,400
Band of the Royal Military College	7,732,401 - 7,733,000
Corps of Military Accountants	7,733,001 - 7,757,000
Royal Army Veterinary Corps	7,757,001 - 7,807,000
Machine Gun Corps disbanded 1922	7,807,001 - 7,868,000
Tank Corps	7,868,001 - 8,109,000

Later blocks of numbers current in the Second World War (which changed the Tank Corps allotment when this became the Royal Tank Regiment under the Royal Armoured Corps) are listed below.

In some cases it had been necessary for new blocks of numbers to be added:

Royal Tank Regiment	7,868,001 - 7,891,868
Royal Armoured Corps	7,891,869 - 8,230,000
Militia	10,000,001 - 10,350,000
Intelligence Corps	10,350,001 - 10,400,000
Royal Army Pay Corps	10,400,001 - 10,500,000
Middle East 2nd Echelon	10,500,001 - 10,508,000
for issue to locally enlisted Allies	
Army Dental Corps	10,510,001 - 10,530,000
Royal Army Ordnance Corps	10,530,001 - 10,600,000
Reconnaissance Corps	10,600,001 - 10,630,000
Army Catering Corps	10,630,001 - 10,655,000
Army Physical Training Corps	10,655,001 - 10,660,000
Royal Army Service Corps	10,660,001 - 11,000,000
Royal Artillery	11,000,000 - 11,500,000
Coast Defence and Anti-Aircraft Branch	
Pioneer Corps	13,000,000 - 14,000,000
Lowland Regiment	14,000,001 - 14,002,500
Highland Regiment	14,002,501 - 14,005,000
General Service Corps	14,200,001 - 15,000,000
India	15,000,001 - 15,005,000
local enlistments into British Regiments and Corps	
Royal Electrical and Mechanical Engineers	16,000,001 - 16,100,000
Non Combatant Corps	97,000,001 - 97,100,000

A new system of army numbering was introduced in August 1947 whereby blocks of numbers were issued in a more random way. This was to counteract the security problem that resulted should a soldier fall into enemy hands, as it was immediately obvious to anybody with a copy of *King's Regulations* which regiment they came from.

If a man leaves the Army and then rejoins he is given a new army number, likewise if he joins the Territorial Army he will also receive a new one.

APPENDIX II

ABBREVIATIONS

A	Acting
	Assistant
A&SH	Argyll and Sutherland Highlanders
AA	Anti Aircraft
	Army Act
AA & CD	Anti Aircraft and Coast Defence
AAC	Army Air Corps
AA COLL	Army Apprentice College
AAHC	Army Auxiliary Horse Company
AAI	Allied Army Italy
AAMC	Australian Army Medical Corps
AARR	Airborne Armoured Reconnaissance Regiment
AAS	Army Apprentices School
AASC	Anti Aircraft Searchlight Company
	Army Air Support Control
AASF	Advanced Air Striking Force
AASL(COY)	Anti Aircraft Searchlight (Company)
AASS	Anti Aircraft Searchlight Section
AATDC	Army Airborne Transport Development Centre
AATE	Anti Aircraft Training Establishment
AB	Army Book
	Airborne
A/B	Airborne
ABC	Armoured Brigade Company (RASC)
ABCA	Army Bureau of Current Affairs
ABOD	Advanced Base Ordnance Depot (India)
ABS	Army Board Secretariat
ABSD	Army Blood Supply Depot (RAMC)

AC	Army Contracts
	Armoured Car
ACC	Army Catering Corps
	Army Cyclist Corps
	Armoured Car Company (RAC)
ACD	Army Chaplain's Department
ACEP	Army Communications Equipment Production
ACI	Army Council Instruction
ACP	Air Composite Platoon (RASC)
A CPL OF HORSE	Acting Corporal of Horse
A CYC CORPS	Army Cyclist Corps
AD	Armoured Division
	Air Despatch
	Assistant Director
	Air Defence
	Ammunition Depot
ADC	Aide-de-Camp
	Army Dental Corps
ADGMS	Assistant Director General of Medical Services
ADMS	Assistant Director Medical Services
ADS	Army Dental Service
	Advanced Dressing Station
ADST	Assistant Director Supply and Transport
ADT	Armoured Division Troops
AE	Army Equipment
AEC	Army Educational Corps
	Army Educational Company
A EDN	Army Education
AEF	American Expeditionary Force
AER	Army Emergency Reserve
AF	Army Form
AFD	Airborne Forces Depot
AFHQ	Allied Forces Headquarters
AFPD	Army Forms and Publications Depot

AFS	Air Formation Signals
AFV	Armoured Fighting Vehicle
AFW	Army Field Workshops
AG	Adjutant General
AGB	Adjutant Generals Base
AGDU	Army Guard Dog Unit
AGR	Army General Reserve
AGRA	Army Group Royal Artillery
AGS	Army Gymnastic Staff
A GYM ST	Army Gymnastic Staff
AH	Army Health
AHC	Army Hospital Corps
AIF	Australian Imperial Force
AIO	Area Intelligence Officer
AIRLINE COY	Airline Company (RE Unit specialising in overhead cables)
AKC	Army Kinema Corporation
A/L	Air Landing
A L/CPL	Acting Lance Corporal
ALFN	Allied Land Forces Norway
ALS	Army Legal Services
AMC	Army Medical Corps
	Airdrome Maintenance Company (RE)
AM COL	Ammunition Column
AMCU	Anti Malarial Control Unit
AMO	Administrative Medical Officer
AMPC	Auxiliary Military Pioneer Corps
AMS	Army Medical Services
	Assistant Military Secretary
AMTD	Advanced Mechanical Transport Depot
A MULE DEPOT	Army Mule Depot
ANS	Army Nursing Services
ANSR	Army Nursing Service Reserve
AO	Army Order
AOC	Army Ordnance Corps
AOD	Army Ordnance Department
	Advanced Ordnance Depot

AOER	Army Officers Emergency Reserve
AOFP	Army Ordnance Field Park
AORE	Army Operational Research Establishment
AOSR	Army Operational Science and Research
AOW	Army Ordnance Workshop
APC	Army Pay Corps
APD	Army Pay Department
APL	Army Pioneers and Labour
APM	Assistant Provost Marshal
APO	Army Post Office
APS	Army Pigeon Service
APSS	Army Printing and Stationary Services
APTC	Army Physical Training Corps
AR	Army Recruiting
ARMD	Armoured
ARRC	Associate of the Royal Red Cross
ARTY	Artillery
ASC	Army Service Corps
	Army Selection Centre
ASCB	Army Sport Control Board
ASD	Army Staff Duties
	Ammunition Sub Depot
A SGT	Acting Sergeant
ASO	Area Searchlight Officer
	Assistant Section Officer
AS OFFH	Army School of Field Hygiene
ASP	Ammunition Sub Park
ASSU	Air Support Signals Unit
A SURG	Army Surgeon
AT	Army Training
	Army Troops
	Anti Tank
ATC	Armoured Training Centre
	Army Troops Company
A T COY	Army Troops Company (RE)
ATS	Auxiliary Territorial Service
ATT	Attached

AUIT	Armoured Unit Initial Training
AVC	Army Veterinary Corps
AVRS	Army Veterinary and Remount Services
AW	Artisan Works (RE)
A WO CL I	Acting Warrant Officer Class I (also Class II and III)
AWOL	Absent Without Leave
AWRE	Atomic Weapons Research Establishment
AYR YEO	Ayrshire Yeomanry
BAC	Brigade Ammunition Column
BAFSV	British Armed Forces Special Vouchers (military currency)
BANU	British Army News Unit
BAOR	British Army of the Rhine (post Second World War)
BAPO	British Army Post Office (RE)
BAR	British Army of the Rhine (post First World War)
BC	Battle Casualty
	Battery Commander
BCD	Biological and Chemical Defence
BCOF	British Commonwealth Occupation Force (Japan)
BD	Bomb Disposal
	Base Depot
	Biological Defence
BDC	Bomb Disposal Company
BDE	Brigade
BDR	Bombardier (Royal Artillery rank of Corporal)
BDS	Bomb Disposal Section (RE)
BDSM	Bandsman
BEDF R	Bedfordshire Regiment
BEDF YEO	Bedfordshire Yeomanry
BEF	British Expeditionary Force
BETFOR	British Element Trieste Force

BFAP	British Forces Aden Protectorate
BFBS	British Forces Broadcasting Service
BFES	British Families' Education Service
BFG	British Forces Germany
BFN	British Forces Network
BFPO	British Forces Post Office
BIO	Brigade Intelligence Officer
BLA	British Liberation Army
BMH	British Military Hospital
BM	Brigade Major
	Beach Master
B/M	Bugle Major
BN	Battalion
BNAF	British North Africa Force
BOD	Base Ordnance Depot
BORD R	Border Regiment
BPTC	Bulk Petrol Transport Company (RASC)
BQMS	Battery Quarter Master Sergeant
BRC	Base Reinforcement Camp
BRCS	British Red Cross Society
BRIG	Brigadier (post 1920)
BRIG GEN	Brigadier General (pre 1920)
BSD	Base Supply Depot (RASC)
BSM	Battery Sergeant Major
BTA	British Troops Austria
BTNI	British Troops in Northern Ireland
BTTN	Battalion
BTU	Blood Transfusion Unit (RAMC)
BTY	Battery
BUCKS YEO	Buckinghamshire Yeomanry
BR WIR	British West Indies Regiment
BWIR	British West Indies Regiment
CA	Civil Affairs
	Coast Artillery
CAMB R	Cambridgeshire Regiment
CAMC	Canadian Army Medical Corps

CAMN HIGHS	Cameron Highlanders
CAPT	Captain
CAS	Coastal Artillery School
CASL	Coast Artillery Searchlight
CAV	Cavalry
CAV BDE	Cavalry Brigade
CB	Confined to Barracks
	Counter Battery
	Commander of the Most Honourable Order of the Bath
CBE	Commander of the Most Excellent Order of the British Empire
CBO	Counter Battery Officer
CC	Chief Censor
	Confined to Camp
CCF	Combined Cadet Force
CCG (BE)	Control Commission Germany (British Element)
CCS	Casualty Clearing Station
CD	Coast Defence
CE	Chief Engineer (RE)
CEF	Canadian Expeditionary Force
CEPO	Civilian Establishment and Pay Officer
CF	Chaplain to the Forces
CFA	Cavalry Field Ambulance
CFN	Craftsman (REME rank of Private)
CG	Chaplain General
	Coldstream Guards
C GDS	Coldstream Guards
CGS	Chief of General Staff
CHES R	Cheshire Regiment
CHES YEO	Cheshire Yeomanry
CIC	Commander in Chief
	Cookery Instruction Centre
	Civilian Internment Camp
CIGS	Chief of the Imperial General Staff
C-IN-C	Commander in Chief

CLC	Chinese Labour Corps
CL YEO	City of London Yeomanry
CMA	Corps of Military Accountants
CMF	Central Mediterranean Force
CMG	Commander of the Order of St Michael and St George
CMP	Corps of Military Police
CMS (AD)	Civilian Medical Services (Army Department)
CO	Commanding Officer
COD	Central Ordnance Depot
C OF AS	Corps of Army Schoolmasters
C OF HRS	Corps of Hussars
C OF LOND YEO	City of London Yeomanry
C OF LRS	Corps of Lancers
COL	Colonel
COMD	Command
	Commander
COMDT	Commandant
COMSEC	Command Secretary
CONN RANG	Connaught Rangers
CO OF LOND YEO	County of London Yeomanry
COY	Company
CPL	Corporal
CQMS	Company Quartermaster Sergeant
CR	Coast Regiment (RA)
CRE	Commander Royal Engineers
CRO	Corps Routine Order
CRS	Corps Rest Station
CRU	Civil Resettlement Unit
CSDIC	Combined Services Detail Interrogation Centre
CSDU	Central Salvage Depot Unit
CSEU	Combined Services Entertainment Unit
C SGT	Colour Sergeant
CSM	Company Sergeant Major
CSR(A)	Chief Superintendent of Ranges (Army)

CT	Clothing and Textiles
	Corps Troops
	Communication Trench
CTBA	Ceased to be Attached
CTBE	Ceased to be Entitled
CTC	Cavalry Tank Corps
CVWW	Council of Voluntary Welfare Workers
CW	Chemical Warfare
D	Director
	Deputy
	Died
D&D	Devon and Dorset Regiment
D&T	Development and Training
DAC	Divisional Ammunition Column
DADAW	Deputy Assistant Director Army Welfare
DADMS	Deputy Assistant Director of Medical Services
DAP	Divisional Ammunition Park
DB	Depot Battalion (RE)
	Depot Brigade (RA)
DC	District Commander
DCC	Defence Communications Centre
DCLI	Duke of Cornwall's Light Infantry
DCM	Distinguished Conduct Medal
	District Court Martial
DCS	District Censorship Station
DDMS	Deputy Director of Medical Services
DE	Duration of Emergency
	Director of Establishment
DEMS	Defensive Equipped Merchant Ship
DENBIGH YEO	Denbighshire Yeomanry
DERR	Duke of Edinburgh's Royal Regiment
DET	Detachment/Detached
DETN	Detention
DEVON R	Devonshire Regiment
DG	Dragoon Guards

D GDS	Dragoon Guards
DGN	Dragoon
DGO	Divisional Gas Officer
DI	Defence Intelligence
DID	Detail Issue Depot (RASC)
DIL	Dangerously Ill List
DIV	Division
DLI	Durham Light Infantry
DMC	Desert Mounted Corps
DMG	Deputy Military Governor
DMR	Drummer
DMS	Driver Mechanic School
DNS	Dragoons
DOC	Docks Operating Company (RE)
D OF CORN L I	Duke of Cornwall's Light Infantry
D OF E	Duration of Engagement
D OF LANCS O Y	Duke of Lancaster's Own Yeomanry
D OF W	Duration of War
	Died of Wounds
DORA	Defence of the Realm Act
DORSET R	Dorset Regiment
DORSET YEO	Dorset Yeomanry
DPM	Deputy Provost Marshal
DR	Despatch Rider
	Driver
	Drummer
DSAF	Depot and School Airborne Forces
DSC	Divisional Supply Column
DSO	Distinguished Service Order
DTR	Driver Training Regiment
DURH L I	Durham Light Infantry
DVR	Driver (rank equating to Private)
DW	Duration of war
	Died of Wounds
E	Echelon
E&M COY	Electrical and Mechanical Company (RE)

EAC	Equipment Assembly Company (REME)
ECC	Emergency Cooks Course
ECH	Echelon
ECT	Emergency Cookery Training
EEF	Egyptian Expeditionary Force
EFC	Expeditionary Force Canteen (First World War)
EFI	Expeditionary Force Institutes
ELC	Egyptian Labour Corps
EME(A)	Electrical and Mechanical Engineering (Army)
EMO	Embarkation Medical Officer
EMS	Emergency Medical Service
ENGR	Engineers
ENSA	Entertainments National Services Association
EOD	Explosive Ordnance Disposal
ERE	Extra Regimental Employment
E R OF YORK Y	East Riding of Yorkshire Yeomanry
ESBD	Electrical Stores Base Depot
	Engineer Store Base Depot
ESD	Engineer Stores Depot
ESE	Engineer Stores Establishment
ESSEX R	Essex Regiment
ESSEX YEO	Essex Yeomanry
EST	Establishments
E SURR R	East Surrey Regiment
E YORK R	East Yorkshire Regiment
EX FCE CAN	Expeditionary Force Canteen
F&F YEO	Fife and Forfar Yeomanry
FA	Field Ambulance
F AMB	Field Ambulance
FANY	First Aid Nursing Yeomanry
FAR	Farrier
FARELF	Far East Land Force
F COY	Fortress Company

FD	Field
FDS	Field Dressing Station
	Forward Delivery Squadron (RAC)
FF REGT	Frontier Force Regiment (India)
FGCM	Field General Court Martial
FH	Field Hospital
FHS	Field Hygiene Section/Station
FLD BKY	Field Bakery
FM	Field Marshal
FMSVF	Federated Malay States Volunteer Force
FOO	Forward Observation Officer
FOU	Forward Observer Unit (RA)
FP	Field Punishment
FPKS	Field Park Squadron (RE)
FPO	Field Post Office
FPS	Field Park Squadron (RE)
FRT	Fortress
FSM	Field Service Manual
FSO	Field Security Officer
FSR	Field Service Regulations
FSS	Field Security Section
FSTC	Field Security Training Centre
FUS	Fusilier (Rank equating to Private)
FVPE	Fighting Vehicle Proving Establishment
FVS	Fighting Vehicle Section
FWN	Forewoman (QMAAC NCO)
G	General Staff
GC	George Cross
GC COY	General Construction Company (RE)
GCM	General Court Martial
GCR	Gold Coast Regiment
GD	General Duties
GDS	Guards
	General Duties Section
GDSM	Guardsman (Rank equating to Private)
GDS M G R	Guards Machine Gun Regiment

GEN	General
GG	Grenadier Guards
G GDS	Grenadier Guards
GH	General Hospital
GHQ	General Headquarters
GLAM YEO	Glamorgan Yeomanry
GLOUC R	Gloucestershire Regiment
GM	George Medal
GMP	Garrison Military Police
GNR	Gunner (Private in Royal Artillery)
GOC	General Officer Commanding
GOC-IN-C	General Officer Commanding-in-Chief
GORD HIGHS	Gordon Highlanders
GORDONS	Gordon Highlanders
GP	Group
GRC	Graves Registration Commission
GRKS	Gurkhas
GRO	General Routine Order
GRU	Graves Registration Unit
GS	General Service
	General Staff
GSC	General Service Corps
GSO	General Staff Officer
GSW	Gun Shot Wound
GT COY	General Transport Company
GTTB	General Trades Training Battalions (Royal Signals)
H&D COY	Holding and Drafting Company
H & R P	Holding and Reconsignment Point
HA	Heavy Artillery
HAA	Heavy Anti Aircraft
HAC	Honourable Artillery Company
H A C ART	Honourable Artillery Company Artillery Section
H A C INF	Honourable Artillery Company Infantry Section

HAMP R	Hampshire Regiment
HAMPS R	Hampshire Regiment
HAMPS YEO	Hampshire Yeomanry
HAT	Home Ambulance Train (RAMC)
HBMGC	Heavy Branch Machine Gun Corps
HCBTC	Home Counties Brigade Training Centre
HD	Home Defence
HE	High Explosive
HEREFORD R	Hereford Regiment
HERT R	Hertfordshire Regiment
HERTS R	Hertfordshire Regiment
HERTS YEO	Hertfordshire Yeomanry
HG	Hotchkiss Gun
	Home Guard
HIGHLAND CYC BN	Highland Cyclist Battalion
HIGH L I	Highland Light Infantry
HKSRGA	Hong Kong and Singapore Royal Garrison Artillery
HKVDC	Hong Kong Volunteer Defence Corps
HLI	Highland Light Infantry
HOUSEHOLD BN	Household Battalion
HPS	Home Port Security (Intelligence Corps)
HQ SW	Headquarters Static Workshop (REME)
HRS	Hussars
	Heavy Recovery Section (REME)
HRS(MT)	Heavy Repair Shop (Motor Transport) (RAOC)
HS	Holding Strength
	Hospital Ship
	Home Service
HSF	Home Service Force
HT	Horse Transport
HTR	Heavy Training Regiment (RAC)
HUNTS CYCLIST BN	Huntingdonshire Cyclist Battalion
I	Intelligence
IA	Indian Army

IACC	Indian Army Corps of Clerks
IAOC	Indian Army Ordnance Corps
IB	Infantry Brigade
IBD	Infantry Base Depot
I/C	In Charge Of
IC	Intelligence Corps
ICC	Intelligence Corps Centre
IE	Inspectorate of Establishments
	Illegal Enlistment
IFCU	Indian Field Censor Unit
IG	Irish Guards
I GDS	Irish Guards
IJLB	Infantry Junior Leader Battalion
INF	Infantry
INFY	Infantry
INT CORPS	Intelligence Corps
IO	Intelligence Officer
IOR	Indian Other Rank
IR GDS	Irish Guards
IS	Imperial Service
ITC	Infantry Training Centre
ITW	Initial Training Wing
IUL	Indian Unattached List (Officers)
I W & D	Inland Waterways and Docks
IWGC	Imperial War Graves Commission
IWP	Instruments and Weapons Production
IWT	Inland Water Transport
JAG	Judge Advocate General
JTC	Junior Training Corps
KA	Killed in Action
KAR	King's African Rifles
KBS	Kite Balloon Section
KEH	King Edward's Horse
K IN A	Killed In Action
KOSB	Kings Own Scottish Borderers

K O SCOT BORD	Kings Own Scottish Borderers
KOYLI	Kings Own Yorkshire Light Infantry
KR	King's Regulations
KRRC	Kings Royal Rifle Corps
K R RIF C	Kings Royal Rifle Corps
KSG	Korea Services Gratuity
KSLI	Kings Shropshire Light Infantry
L	Labour
	Lance
LAA	Light Anti Aircraft
LABOUR C	Labour Corps
LAC	London Assembly Centre
LAD	Light Aid Detachment
LANARK YEO	Lanarkshire Yeomanry
LAN FUS	Lancashire Fusiliers
LC	Labour Corps
L CPL	Lance Corporal
L/CPL	Lance Corporal
LCRS	Lancers
LDAC	London District Assembly Centre
LDRD	London District Reception Depot (RAC)
LDV	Local Defence Volunteers
LDY OP	Laundry Operator (RAOC)
LEE	London Electrical Engineers
LEIC R	Leicestershire Regiment
LEIC YEO	Leicestershire Yeomanry
LEINS R	Leinster Regiment
LF	Lancashire Fusiliers
LG	Life Guards
	Lewis Gun
L GDS	Life Guards
LIAP	Leave in addition to Python
LIEUT	Lieutenant
LINC R	Lincolnshire Regiment
LINC YEO	Lincolnshire Yeomanry
LIR	London Irish Rifles

LMB FA	Lowland Mounted Brigade Field Ambulance (RAMC)
L N LAN R	Loyal North Lancashire Regiment
LO	Liaison Officer
LOA	Local Overseas Allowance
LOC	Lines of Communication
L OF C	Lines of Communication
LOND R	London Regiment
LOTH & BORD H	Lothian and Border Horse
LOVAT'S SCTS	Lovat's Scouts
L'POOL R	Liverpool Regiment
LR	Light Railway
LRB	London Rifle Brigade
LRDG	Long Range Desert Group
LRS	Lancers
	Light Repair Section
LS	Land Service
LS & GC	Long Service and Good Conduct
L SGT	Lance Sergeant
LSL	Long Service List
LT	Lieutenant
	Line Telegraphy
LT COL	Lieutenant Colonel
LT GEN	Lieutenant General
LTM	Light Trench Mortar
LTMB	Light Trench Mortar Battery
LTR	Long Term Reserve
LWOP	Leave without Pay
M	Medical
	Movement
MA	Military Adviser
	Military Assistant
	Military Attache
MAC	Motor Ambulance Convoy
MAD	Military Accounts Department
MAJ	Major

MAJ GEN	Major General
MANCH R	Manchester Regiment
MB	Mercian Brigade
	Medical Board
MBU	Mobile Bath Unit (Pioneer Corps)
MC	Military Cross
	Movement Control
	Motor Cycle
MCU	Military Collection Unit
MDC	Mobile Defence Corps
MD COY	Motor Driver Company (ATS)
MDS	Main Dressing Station
ME COY	Mechanical Equipment Company
MEF	Mediterranean Expeditionary Force
MELF	Middle East Land Force
MEP	Mechanical Equipment Park Company (RE)
MET	Meteorological
MEXE	Military Engineering Experimental Establishment
MFO	Military Forwarding Officer
MFP	Military Foot Police
MGC	Machine Gun Corps
MGC CAV	Machine Gun Corps Cavalry
M G CORPS	Machine Gun Corps
MGO	Master General of the Ordnance
MG TC	Machine Gun Training Centre
MID	Mention in Despatches
MIDD'X R	Middlesex Regiment
MIRS	Military Intelligence Research Section
MLO	Military Landing Officer
MLU	Mobile Laundry Unit (RAOC)
MM	Military Medal
MMGC	Motor Machine Gun Corps
MMGS	Motor Machine Gun Service
MMP	Military Mounted Police
MO	Medical Officer
	Military Operations

MOB	Mobilisation
MOD	Ministry of Defence
MONMOUTH R	Monmouthshire Regiment
MOV	Movement
MP	Manpower
	Military Police
MP&DB	Military Prison and Detention Barracks
MPDB	Military Provost Detention Barracks
MPFC	Mobile Petrol Filling Company
MPSC	Military Provost Staff Corps
MPTC	Mobile Petrol Transport Company
MR	Mounted Rifles
MRA	Maritime Royal Artillery
MRE	Microbiological Research Establishment
MRS	Medical Reception Station
MSD	Main Supply Depot (RAOC)
MSG	Maintenance Support Group
MSM	Meritorious Service Medal
MT	Mechanical Transport
	Military Transport
MT BN	Motor Training Battalion
MTF	Mauritius Territorial Force
MTO	Mechanical Transport Officer
MTS	Motor Transport Stores
MTTD	Motor Transport Training Depot
MU	Maintenance Unit
MWEE	Mechanical Warfare Experimental Establishment
MX	Middlesex Regiment
NAAFI	Navy, Army and Air Force Institutes
NACB	Navy and Army Canteen Board
NATO	North Atlantic Treaty Organisation
NBC	Nuclear, Biological and Chemical Warfare
NCC	Non Combatant Corps
NCO	Non-Commissioned Officer
N CYC BN	Northern Cyclist Battalion

NDC	National Defence Company
NDS	Northumbria District Signals
NEI	Netherlands (Dutch) East Indies
NF	Northumberland Fusiliers
NIB	North Irish Brigade
NID	North Irish Depot
NIM	North Irish Militia
N IR H	North Irish Horse
NK	Not Known
NO	Nursing Orderly
NOK	Next of Kin
NORF R	Norfolk Regiment
NORF YEO	Norfolk Yeomanry
NORTH'D FUS	Northumberland Fusiliers
NORTH'D YEO	Northumberland Yeomanry
NORTH'N R	Northamptonshire Regiment
NORTH'N YEO	Northamptonshire Yeomanry
N SOM YEO	North Somerset Yeomanry
NSRW	National Service Reserve Wing
N STAFF R	North Staffordshire Regiment
NYD	Not Yet Diagnosed
NZAMC	New Zealand Army Medical Corps
O	Operations
OAC	Ordnance Ammunition Company
OBE	Order of the British Empire
OBLI	Oxfordshire and Buckinghamshire Light Infantry
OC	Officer Commanding
	Officer Cadet
OCA	Old Comrades Association
OCTU	Officer Cadet Training Unit
OD	Ordnance Depot
OF	Ordnance Factories
OFC	Operator Fire Control (RA)
OFP	Ordnance Field Park
OIC	Officer in Charge

OP	Observation Post
OPWC	Overseas Prisoner of War Camp
OR	Other Rank
ORD	Ordnance
ORS	Operational Research Section
ORTU	Other Ranks Training Unit
OTC	Officers Training Corps
OWL	Operator Wireless and Line
OX & BUCKS L I	Oxfordshire and Buckinghamshire Light Infantry
OXF YEO	Oxfordshire Yeomanry
P&SS	Printing and Stationery Service
PAIFORCE	Persia and Iraq Force
PARA REGT	Parachute Regiment
PCC	Port Construction Company
	Postal and Courier Communications
PCLU	Pioneer and Civil Labour Unit
P CORPS	Pioneer Corps
PD	Petrol Depot
PDC	Physical Development Centre
PEE	Proof and Experimental Establishment
PEMBROKE YEO	Pembrokeshire Yeomanry
PK	Park
PL	Platoon
PLK	Princess Louise's Kensington Regiment
P/M	Pipe Major
PM	Provost Marshal
PMC	President of the Mess Committee
PMR	Paymaster
	Practical Map Reading
PNE	Permanently Non Effective
PNR	Pioneer
POC	Port Operating Company
POW	Prisoner of War
P PARK	Petrol Park
PRP	Petrol Refilling Point

PRRB	Parachute Regiment Reserve Battalion
PSC	Passed Staff College
PSM	Platoon Sergeant Major
PSP	Petrol Stores Platoon
PTC	Primary Training Corps
PTE	Private
PTFOC	Petrol Tin Factory Operating Company (RASC)
PTW	Primary Training Wing
PU	Permanently Unfit
PUO	Pyrexia of Unknown Origin
PVO	Principal Veterinary Officer
PW	Prisoner of War
PWV	South Lancashire Regiment (Prince of Wales's Volunteers)
Q	Quartering
QAIMNS	Queen Alexandra's Imperial Military Nursing Service
QAIMNS(R)	Queen Alexandra's Imperial Military Nursing Service Reserve
QARANC	Queen Alexandra's Royal Army Nursing Corps
QM	Quartermaster
QMAAC	Queen Mary's Army Auxiliary Corps
QMG	Quartermaster General
QMS	Quartermaster Sergeant
QOR GLASGOW YEO	Queen's Own Royal Glasgow Yeomanry
QR	Queen's Regulations
QUEENS S R	Queen's Royal West Surrey Regiment
R	Reconnaissance
RA	Royal Artillery
RAC	Royal Armoured Corps
RACD	Royal Army Chaplains Department
RAChD	Royal Army Chaplains Department
RACR	Royal Armoured Corps Range

RADC	Royal Army Dental Corps
RAEC	Royal Army Education Corps
RAF	Royal Air Force
RAMC	Royal Army Medical Corps
RAOC	Royal Army Ordnance Corps
RAP	Regimental Aid Post
RAPC	Royal Army Pay Corps
RASC	Royal Army Service Corps
RATA	Royal Army Temperance Association
RAVC	Royal Army Veterinary Corps
RB	Rifle Brigade
RBC	Reinforcement Base Depot
R BERKS R	Royal Berkshire Regiment
RC	Roman Catholic
	Reconnaissance Corps
RC COY	Railway Construction Company (RE)
RCM	Regimental Court Martial
RCT	Royal Corps of Transport
RDC	Royal Defence Corps
RDD	Reception and Discharge Depot
R DEVON YEO	Royal Devon Yeomanry
RDF	Royal Dublin Fusiliers
R D FUS	Royal Dublin Fusiliers
R DUB FUS	Royal Dublin Fusiliers
RE	Royal Engineers
REGT	Regiment
R E KENT YEO	Royal East Kent Yeomanry
REME	Royal Electrical and Mechanical Engineers
REPS	Royal Engineers Postal Section
RES	Reserve
RET	Retired
RF	Royal Fusiliers
RFA	Royal Field Artillery
RFC	Royal Flying Corps
RFN	Rifleman (Rank equating to Private)
R FUS	Royal Fusiliers

RGA	Royal Garrison Artillery
RGBW	Royal Gloucestershire, Berkshire and Wiltshire Regiment
RGH	Royal Gloucestershire Hussars
RGJ	Royal Green Jackets
RGT	Regiment
R GUERNSEY L I	Royal Guernsey Light Infantry
RHA	Royal Horse Artillery
	Reserve Heavy Artillery
RHE	Return to Home Establishment
RHF	Royal Highland Fusiliers
RHG	Royal Horse Guards
R H GDS	Royal Horse Guards
R HIGHRS	Royal Highlanders (Black Watch)
RHQ	Regimental Headquarters
RHU	Reinforcement Holding Unit
RIC	Royal Irish Constabulary
RIF	Royal Irish Fusiliers
RIF BRIG	Rifle Brigade
R INNIS FUS	Royal Inniskilling Fusiliers
R IR FUS	Royal Irish Fusiliers
R IR REG	Royal Irish Regiment
R IR RIF	Royal Irish Rifles
R LANC R	Royal Lancaster Regiment
RM	Royal Marines
	Remount
RMA	Royal Military Academy (Woolwich until 1947)
	Royal Marine Artillery
	Royal Malta Artillery
RMAS	Royal Military Academy Sandhurst
RMC	Royal Military College (Sandhurst)
RMF	Royal Munster Fusiliers
RMLI	Royal Marine Light Infantry
RMO	Regimental Medical Officer
RMP	Royal Military Police
R MUNS FUS	Royal Munster Fusiliers

RMW	Railway Mobile Workshop
RND	Royal Naval Division (from 1916, 63rd Division)
R N DEVON YEO	Royal North Devon Yeomanry
RO	Recruiting Officer
	Retired Officer
	Reconnaissance Officer
	Routine Order
ROC	Railway Operating Company
ROD	Railway Operating Division (RE)
ROF	Royal Ordnance Factory
R OF O	Reserve Of Officers
RP	Regimental Police
RPC	Royal Pioneer Corps
RPM	Rounds Per Minute
RQMS	Regimental Quartermaster Sergeant
RRC	Royal Red Cross
RRF	Royal Regiment of Fusiliers
R R OF CAV	Royal Regiment of Cavalry
RS	Royal Scots
RSAF	Royal Small Arms Factory
RSC	Recruit Selection Centre
R SC FUS	Royal Scots Fusiliers
R SCOTS	Royal Scots
R S FUS	Royal Scots Fusiliers
R SIGNALS	Royal Signals
R SIGS	Royal Signals
RSM	Regimental Sergeant Major
RSR	Raiding Support Regiment
R SUSS R	Royal Sussex Regiment
R/T	Radio Telephony
RTC	Royal Tank Corps
RTO	Railway Transport Officer
	Railway Traffic Officer
RTR	Royal Tank Regiment
RTU	Returned To Unit
RUR	Royal Ulster Rifles

RW	Royal Warrant
R WAR R	Royal Warwickshire Regiment
RWF	Royal Welsh Fusiliers (from 1920, Welch)
R W FUS	Royal Welsh Fusiliers
RWK	Queen's Own Royal West Kent Regiment
R W KENT R	Royal West Kent Regiment
RY(S)	Railway(s)
S	Service
	Supply
S&M	Sappers and Miners
S&T	Supply and Transport
SANLC	South African Native Labour Corps
SARB	Siege Artillery Reserve Brigade
S ARMS SCH	Small Arms School
SAS	Special Air Service
SASC	Small Arms School Corps
SA SCHOOL	Small Arms School
SBAC	Siege Battery Ammunition Column
SCD	Stores and Clothing Department
SCO H	Scottish Horse
SCO RIF	Scottish Rifles (Cameronians)
SCU	Special Communications Unit (Royal Signals)
SD	Staff Duties
SDF	Sudan Defence Force
SDR	Special Despatch Rider
SEAC	South East Asia Command
SEA HIGHRS	Seaforth Highlanders
SEALF	South East Asia Land Force
SEATO	South East Asia Treaty Organisation
SEE	Signals Experimental Establishment
SEL	School of Electric Lighting
SG	Scots Guards
S GDS	Scots Guards
SGE	Siege
SGT	Sergeant

SH	Seaforth Highlanders
SHAEF	Supreme Headquarters Allied Expeditionary Force
SHAPE	Supreme Headquarters Allied Powers Europe
SHER RANG	Sherwood Rangers
SHROPS L I	Shropshire Light Infantry
SHROPS YEO	Shropshire Yeomanry
SI(A)	Services Intelligence (Army)
SIB	Special Investigations Branch
SIG	Signalman (Rank equating to Private in Royal Signals)
SIGMN	Signalman
S IR H	South Irish Horse
SIS	Security Identification Section
SIW	Self Inflicted Wound
SJT	Serjeant
SL	Searchlight
S LAN R	South Lancashire Regiment
SLDS	Searchlight Directing Station
SLE	Searchlight Emplacement
SLER	Searchlight Engine Room
SLI	Somerset Light Infantry
SLL	Searchlight Laying
SLT	Searchlight Training
SM	Sergeant Major
SME	School of Military Engineering
S MJR	Sergeant Major
SMO	Senior Medical Officer
SNLR	Services No Longer Required
SO	Staff Officer
	Signal Officer
	Section Officer
SOE	Special Operations Executive
S OF A	School of Artillery
S OF M	School of Musketry
SOM L I	Somerset Light Infantry

SOS	Struck Off Strength
	Static Officers Shop
SPR	Sapper (Private in Royal Engineers)
SQN	Squadron
SR	Special Reserve
	Supplementary Reserve
	Sound Ranging
SRD	Supply Reserve Depot
SRS	Sound Ranging Section
SS	Stationery Service
SSB	Special Services Brigade
S/SGT	Staff Sergeant
S STAFF R	South Staffordshire Regiment
SSVF	Straits Settlements Volunteer Force
ST	Supply and Transport (RASC)
STAFF YEO	Staffordshire Yeomanry
STC	Signal Training Centre
	Special Training Centre
	Survey Training Centre
	Senior Training Corps
SU	Salvage Unit
SUFF R	Suffolk Regiment
SUFF YEO	Suffolk Yeomanry
SURR YEO	Surrey Yeomanry
SVC	Shanghai Volunteer Corps
SVY	Survey
SW	Static Workshop (REME)
S WALES BORD	South Wales Borderers
SWB	Silver War Badge
	South Wales Borderers
SWH	Scottish Women's Hospitals
T	Transport
TA	Territorial Army
TANS	Territorial Army Nursing Service
TAVR	Territorial Army Volunteer Reserve

TB	Training Battalion
	Tank Brigade
	Telegraph Battalion
TC	Troop Commander
	Training Corps
	Traffic Control
TCC	Traffic Control Company
TCO	Train Conducting Officer
T COY	Tunnelling Company
TCP	Traffic Control Post
TD	Territorial Decoration
	Tractor Drawn
TDS	Tank Delivery Squadron
TE	Training Establishment
TEE	Tyne Electrical Engineers
TF	Territorial Force
TFNS	Territorial Force Nursing Service
TK	Tank
TLC	Tank Landing Craft
TM	Trench Mortar
TMB	Trench Mortar Battery
TN	Transportation
TO	Transport Officer
TOS	Taken on Strength
TP	Troop
TP CG COY	Troop Carrying Company (RASC)
TPR	Trooper
TPS	Troops
TPTR	Trumpeter
TR	Training Reserve
TRB	Training Reserve Brigade
TRG	Training
TSM	Troop Sergeant Major
UM	Unit Mobilisation
UN	United Nations
UOTC	University Officers Training Corps

V	Veterinary
VAD	Voluntary Aid Detachment
VC	Victoria Cross
VCP	Vehicle Collection Point
VD	Venereal Disease
	Volunteer Decoration
VES	Veterinary Evacuating Station
VO	Veterinary Officer
VP	Vulnerable Points (CMP)
VPP	Volunerable Points Provost (CMP)
VRD	Vehicle Reserve/Reception Depot
V/S	Visual Signalling
V/T	Visual Telegraphy
VTC	Volunteer Training Corps
WAAC	Women's Army Auxiliary Corps
W AFR R	West African Regiment
WE	War Establishment
WEF	With Effect From
WELSH H	Welsh Horse
WELSH HC	Welsh Hospital Corps
WELSH R	Welsh Regiment
WEST & CUMB Y	Westmoreland and Cumberland Yeomanry
WG	Welsh Guards
W GDS	Welsh Guards
WGNR	Waggoner (Army Service Corps)
WHC	Women's Hospital Corps
WI	Wireless Intelligence
WILTS R	Wiltshire Regiment
WILTS YEO	Wiltshire Yeomanry
WIR	West India Regiment
W KENT YEO	West Kent Yeomanry
WKR	Worker (grade equating to Private in QMAAC)
WO	War Office
	Warrant Officer
W O CL I	Warrant Officer Class I (also Class II and III)

WORC R	Worcestershire Regiment
WORC YEO	Worcestershire Yeomanry
WOSB	War Office Selection Board
WRAC	Women's Royal Army Corps
W RID R	West Riding Regiment
W/S	War Substantive
W SOM YEO	West Somerset Yeomanry
WT	Weapon Training
W/T	Wireless Telegraphy
WT COY	Water Tank Company (RASC)
WWCP	Walking Wounded Collecting Post
W YORK R	West Yorkshire Regiment
YEO	Yeomanry
Y & L R	York and Lancaster Regiment
YD	Yorkshire Dragoons
YH	Yorkshire Hussars
YORK DNS	Yorkshire Dragoons
YORK HRS	Yorkshire Hussars
YORK & LANC R	York and Lancaster Regiment
YORK R	Yorkshire Regiment
YORKS L I	Yorkshire Light Infantry
YS	Young Soldier
ZION MULE C	Zion Mule Corps
ZMC	Zion Mule Corps

APPENDIX III

CONSCRIPTION

The British Army has traditionally been one which relies on men volunteering rather than being forced to serve. However, during the twentieth century there were several periods when conscription was in place, and this appendix attempts to give a brief view of this complex issue.

FIRST WORLD WAR

On the outbreak of the First World War it was immediately apparent that the Regular Army and mobilised Territorial battalions would not be sufficient. Kitchener launched his famous appeal for more men and soon the 'First Hundred Thousand' were recruited to be followed by four more. These were volunteers who signed on to serve for 'three years or the duration', many of whom formed the 'Pals' battalions, and they were often known as the New Armies or Kitchener's Armies. However, after the initial surge of enthusiasm, the numbers of those volunteering declined to such a level that much debate was given to introducing conscription.

In July 1915 a National Registration Act was passed, which required everybody between the age of 15 and 65 to register. This showed that there were large numbers of men who were not involved in essential warwork; for example, employment in the areas of munitions, agriculture, mining, railways, etc. In October 1915 Lord Derby was appointed Director-General of Recruiting and introduced the Derby Scheme which was in operation until mid-December 1915. This allowed men to volunteer or to attest their willingness to serve at a later date. The men who attested were divided into those who were single, who were to be called up first, and those who were married. There were also divisions into 23 different age 'Groups' between 18 and 41. The scheme showed that large numbers of single men had still not volunteered or attested, and reluctantly conscription was introduced in 1916 (this did not apply to Ireland).

The first Military Service Act came into effect in January 1916 and this conscripted all single men and widowers without children aged between 18 and 41. In May 1916 this was extended to all men in this age range including those who were married. A man could be exempted because of his occupation or health and some men were conscientious objectors. Other Military Service Acts followed: April 1917 saw the Military Service (Review of Exemptions) Act which restricted industrial, agricultural and mining exemptions and lowered fitness standards; the Military Service (Conventions with Allied States) Act of July 1917 allowed the conscription of British subjects living abroad and of Allied citizens living in Great Britain (conventions were signed with Russia in July and France in October); the Military Service Act of February 1918 allowed the removal of more exemptions; and the second Military Service Act of April 1918 conscripted men between the ages of 41 and 50 (it included an allowance for this to be extended to 56 with further exemptions if necessary and it also allowed for the extension of conscription to Ireland); and finally, the Naval, Military and Air Force Service Act of April 1919 retained compulsory military service until 30 April 1920, although the conscription of new recruits ceased at midday on 11 November 1918.

SECOND WORLD WAR

When it began to look as if conflict would be inevitable, various schemes came into effect to prepare adequate manpower for the Second World War. A Schedule of Reserved Occupations was drawn up in January 1939 by the Ministry of Labour. Although this was later to become more comprehensive and various changes were to be made in following years, it did go some way to setting out who would be exempt from military service and signified a more organised approach to obtaining men for the Armed Forces. In March 1939 plans were made to double the numbers in the Territorial Army. Although this was a purely voluntary service numbers had increased from around 204,000 in January 1939 to 428,000 at the end of August 1939.

In May 1939 the Military Training Act came into effect. This meant that all men on reaching the age of 20 had to join the Army, Royal Navy or Royal Air Force. They were allowed to choose which branch of service to join – those who joined the Army became known as Militiamen. This was to involve six months full-time service, with three and a half years on the Reserve with liability for training every year. About 34,000 men joined under this scheme in the first intake on 15 July 1939 and recruits were to be taken on at intervals of two months. In fact the July intake was to be the last under this scheme as the Second World War broke out and the National Service Act came into effect on 6 September 1939. This called for conscription of all males between the ages of 18 and 41.

A second act was passed in December 1941 which extended conscription to women, and made some additional amendments, for example raising the upper age limit for men to 51. Men from Northern Ireland were to be exempt from conscription.

NATIONAL SERVICE

The need for large numbers to serve in the Armed Forces did not decline with the end of the Second World War. After the fighting had ceased in Europe large numbers of men were required in the Far East, and later were involved in keeping the peace and in the withdrawal from Empire. It was decided in 1947 that National Service should continue and the National Service Acts consolidated the Second World War legislation for men aged between 18 and 26. From 1 January 1949 National Servicemen were liable to serve for a period of eighteen months, with four years in the Reserve, although this was later increased to two years, with three and a half years in the Reserve, owing to the outbreak of the Korean War in 1950. By 1951 National Service men made up 50% of the Army's manpower, but continued conscription was not universally popular and there were constant calls to abolish it. It was possible for call-up to be deferred and there were a number of reserved occupations.

The rearming of West Germany and the development of an independent nuclear deterrent allowed Britain to reduce its Armed Forces. The call up for National Service ceased on 31 December 1960 although it was not until 1963 that the last National Serviceman left the Army. There are two contenders for the last man to complete National Service; Private Fred Turner of the Army Catering Corps, attached to the 13th/18th Hussars, had the number 23819209 and was discharged on 7 May 1963, whilst Lieutenant Richard Vaughan of the Royal Army Pay Corps left his unit in Germany on 4 May 1963 but was not officially discharged until 13 May.

APPENDIX IV

ADDRESSES

The addresses below contain varying elements of information. Most of the Ministry of Defence offices will only deal with enquiries by post, (although sometimes there is the initial possibility of making contact by telephone or e-mail – where this is the case, the relevant details are given). It is not possible to visit some addresses in person, and those which are accessible to the public will often need readers' tickets to gain admittance. Please note that it is always advisable to contact an institution in advance of your intended visit to find out how your objectives can best be achieved, to check that they have what you want to see and will be open at the time you would like to visit. It is also helpful to enclose a stamped addressed envelope when writing to institutions and associations.

The National Archives
Ruskin Avenue, Kew, Richmond, Surrey TW9 4DU
Tel: 020 8876 3444
www.nationalarchives.gov.uk

Army Personnel Centre
Disclosures 4, MP 400, Kentigern House, 65 Brown Street, Glasgow G2 8EX
Tel: 0845 600 9963
E-mail: disc4.civsec@apc.army.mod.uk

Regimental Headquarters Grenadier Guards/Coldstream Guards/Scots Guards/Irish Guards/Welsh Guards
Wellington Barracks, Birdcage Walk, London SW1E 6HQ
Postal enquiries only

Ministry of Defence Medal Office

Building 250, RAF Innsworth, Gloucester GL3 1HW

Tel: 0141 224 3600

Armed Forces Personnel Administration Agency (JPAC)

Joint Casualty and Compassionate Centre, Building 182, RAF Innsworth, Gloucester GL3 1HW

Postal enquiries only

Commonwealth War Graves Commission

2 Marlow Road, Maidenhead, Berkshire SL6 7DX

Tel: 01628 634221

www.cwgc.org

National Army Museum

Royal Hospital Road, Chelsea, London SW3 4HT

Tel: 020 7730 0717

www.national-army-museum.ac.uk

Family Records Centre

1 Myddelton Street, London EC1R 1UW

Tel: 020 8392 5300   Fax: 020 8487 9214

www.familyrecords.gov.uk/frc/

General Register Office

PO Box 2, Southport, Merseyside PR8 2JD

Tel: 0845 603 7788

www.gro.gov.uk

General Register Office for Scotland

New Register House, 3 West Register Street, Edinburgh, Scotland EH1 3YT

Tel: 0131 314 4433

www.gro-scotland.gov.uk/

General Register Office (Northern Ireland)

Oxford House, 49-55 Chichester Street, Belfast BT1 4HL

Tel: 028 9025 2000

www.groni.gov.uk

General Register Office (Dublin)

Government Offices, Convent Road, Roscommon, Eire

Tel: 090 663 2900

www.groireland.ie/

British Library Newspaper Library

Colindale Avenue, London NW9 5HE

Tel: 020 7412 7353   Fax: 020 7412 7379

www.bl.uk/collections/newspapers.html

British Library

96 Euston Road, London NW1 2DB

Tel: 020 7412 7332

www.bl.uk

Guildhall Library

Aldermanbury, London EC2P 2EJ

Tel: 020 7332 1868

www.cityoflondon.gov.uk/Corporation/leisure_heritage

Society of Genealogists

14 Charterhouse Buildings, Goswell Road, London EC1M 7BA

Publishes *Genealogists Magazine*

Tel: 020 7251 8799   Fax: 020 7250 1800

www.sog.org.uk

Federation of Family History Societies
c/o FFHS Administrator, PO Box 2425, Coventry CV5 6YX
Publishes *Family History News and Digest: the Official Journal of the Federation of Family History Societies*
www.ffhs.org.uk

Family Tree Magazine
ABM Publishing Ltd, 61 Great Whyte, Ramsey, Huntingdon, Cambridgeshire PE26 1HJ
Tel: 01487 814050   Fax: 01487 711361
www.family-tree.co.uk

Royal British Legion
48 Pall Mall, London SW1Y 5JY
Publishes *Legion Magazine*
Tel: 08457 725 725
www.britishlegion.org.uk

Ancestors
PO Box 38, Richmond TW9 4AJ
www.ancestorsmagazine.co.uk

Family History Monthly
The Metropolis Group, 140 Wales Farm Road, London W3 6UG
www.metropolis.co.uk/familyhistory.html

Soldier
Ordnance Road, Aldershot, Hampshire GU11 2DU
www.soldiermagazine.co.uk

Orders and Medals: the Journal of the Orders and Medals Research Society
PO Box 1904, Southam, CV47 2ZX
www.omrs.org.uk

British Association for Cemeteries in South Asia
76 1/2 Chartfield Avenue, London SW15 6HQ
www.bacsa.org.uk

United Kingdom National Inventory of War Memorials
Imperial War Museum, Lambeth Road, London SE1 6HZ
Tel: 020 7207 9851/9863   Fax: 020 7207 9859
www.ukniwm.org.uk

SOME USEFUL WEB-SITES AND REGIMENTAL ASSOCIATIONS

The best source for regimental museum addresses is the 10th edition of Wise's *A Guide to Military Museums*. This section seeks to provide addresses for some regimental associations which may otherwise prove difficult to track down, and also web-sites which may prove helpful.

Gallipoli Association
PO Box 26907, London SE21 8WB
www.gallipoli-association.org

Machine Gun Corps Old Comrades Association
c/o Honorary Secretary, Penfro, 111 Main Street, Pembroke SA71 4DB
Tel: 01646 682753 [contact by telephone preferred]
www.machineguncorps.co.uk

Salonika Campaign Society
c/o Chairman Alan Wakefield, 4 Watsons Walk, St Albans, Hertfordshire
AL1 1PA
www.salonika.freeserve.co.uk

Western Front Association

c/o Membership Secretary John Richardson, 12 Malton Road, Heaton Moor, Stockport, Cheshire SK4 4DE

www.westernfront.co.uk

16th Irish Division

http://freespace.virgin.net/sh.k/xvidiv.html

ARCHON (Archives Online)

www.nationalarchives.gov.uk/archon

Army Museums Ogilby Trust

www.armymuseums.org.uk

Britain's Small Wars

www.britains-smallwars.com

British Army

www.army.mod.uk

Combined Irish Regiments Association

www.combined-irish-regiments-oca.co.uk

Connaught Rangers Regimental Association

c/o King House Museum, Boyle, County Roscommon, Eire

Cyndi's List

www.cyndislist.com

Familia: the UK and Ireland's Guide to Genealogical Resources in Public Libraries

www.familia.org.uk

Familyrecords.gov.uk Consortium

www.familyrecords.gov.uk

Forces Reunited

www.forcesreunited.org.uk

GENUKI: UK & Ireland Genealogy

www.genuki.org.uk

Labour Corps 1917-1921

www.geocities.com/labour_corps

Land Forces of Britain, the Empire and Commonwealth

www.regiments.org

London Gazette

www.gazettes-online.co.uk

The Long, Long Trail: the British Army in the Great War

www.1914-1918.net

The Military Heritage of Ireland Trust

www.irishsoldiers.com

Ministry of Defence

www.mod.uk

MOD Reunited

www.modreunited.com

National Register of Archives

www.nationalarchives.gov.uk/nra

Royal Dublin Fusiliers Association

The Dublin Civic Museum, 58 South William Street, Dublin 2, Eire

www.greatwar.ie

Royal Munster Fusiliers Association

www.rmfa92.org/

Royal Pioneer Corps Association

www.royalpioneercorps.co.uk

Scots at War Trust

www.fettes.com/scotsatwar/

Veterans Agency

www.veteransagency.mod.uk

All contact details in this publication were correct at the time of printing.

APPENDIX V

SELECT BIBLIOGRAPHY

All of these books are held by the Department of Printed Books and can be consulted by making an appointment at least 24 hours in advance of your visit. Alternative copies may be available through the inter-library loan scheme - please enquire at your local library. Some titles will be out of print and you should be aware that second hand military books are highly sought after and are likely to be very expensive to purchase (although there is a growing market in facsimile reprints).

The bibliography is divided into helpful reference books and guides for family historians (p. 116); general books on army structure, organisation and life (p. 120); medals (p. 130); rolls of honour (p. 134); medical histories (p. 135); trench maps (p. 136); battlefield guides (p. 136); and military wives and children (p. 138).

HELPFUL BOOKS FOR FAMILY HISTORIANS

BECKETT, Ian FW
The First World War: the Essential Guide to Sources in the UK National Archives
by Ian FW Beckett.
Public Record Office, Richmond, Surrey, 2002; xvi, 288pp; ill.
ISBN 1-903365-41-4

BEVAN, Amanda

Tracing Your Ancestors in the Public Record Office by Amanda Bevan.
6th ed.; Public Record Office, Richmond, Surrey, 2002; xviii, 524pp; ill., facsim., figs.
(Public Record Office Handbook; no. 19)
ISBN 1-903365-34-1

BLATCHFORD, Robert

The Family and Local History Handbook: incorporating the Genealogical Services Directory edited and compiled by Robert Blatchford.
9th ed.; Robert Blatchford Publishing, York, 2005; pbk.
ISBN 0-9530297-8-6

CANTWELL, John D

The Second World War: a Guide to Documents in the Public Record Office by John D Cantwell.
3rd rev. ed.; Public Record Office, Richmond, Surrey, 1998; ix, 299pp.
(Public Record Office Handbook; no. 15)
ISBN 1-873162-60-X

COLWELL, Stella

The Family Records Centre: a User's Guide by Stella Colwell.
2nd ed.; Public Record Office, Richmond, Surrey, 2002; xvi, 176pp; ill., facsims., plan.
(Public Record Office Readers' Guide; no. 17)
ISBN 1-903365-36-8

FOWLER, Simon

Army Records for Family Historians by Simon Fowler and William Spencer.
2nd rev. ed.; Public Record Office, Richmond, Surrey, 1998; xiv, 154pp; ill., facsims., col. frontis; pbk.
(Public Record Office Readers' Guide; no. 2)
ISBN 1-873162-59-6

FOWLER, Simon

Tracing Your First World War Ancestors by Simon Fowler.

Countryside Books, Newbury, Berkshire, 2003; 144pp; ill., facsims.; pbk.

ISBN 1-85306-791-1

HOLDING, Norman

World War I Army Ancestry by Norman Holding.

3rd ed.; Federation of Family History Societies (Publications), Birmingham, 1997; 95pp; ill., facsims.; pbk.

ISBN 1-86006-056-2

HOLDING, Norman

More Sources of World War I Army Ancestry by Norman Holding.

3rd ed.; Federation of Family History Societies (Publications), Bury, Lancashire, 1998; 102pp; ill., facsims., figs.; pbk.

ISBN 1-86006-083-8

HOLDING, Norman

The Location of British Army Records, 1914-1918 by Norman Holding, revised and updated by Iain Swinnerton.

4th ed.; Federation of Family History Societies (Publications), Bury, Lancashire, 1999; 120pp; ill., facsims.; pbk.

ISBN 1-86006-084-6

LAKE, FH

A List of Regimental Journals and other Serial Publications of the British Army . . . by FH Lake.

N. pub., n. p., 1983; 10, 231 leaves.

ROPER, Michael

The Records of the War Office and Related Departments, 1660-1964 by Michael Roper.

Public Record Office, Richmond, Surrey, 1998; xiv, 364pp; 16pp of plates; ill., facsims., col. frontis.; pbk.

(Public Record Office Handbook; no. 29)

ISBN 1-873-162-45-6

SPENCER, William

Army Service Records of the First World War by William Spencer.

3rd rev. ed.; Public Record Office, Richmond, Surrey, 2001; xvi, 112pp; ill., facsims., col. frontis., ports.; pbk.

(Public Record Office Readers' Guide; no. 19)

ISBN 1-903365-55-3

SPENCER, William

Records of the Militia and Volunteer Forces, 1757-1945: including Records of the Volunteers, Rifle Volunteers, Yeomanry, Imperial Yeomanry, Fencibles, Territorials and the Home Guard revised and updated by William Spencer.

2nd rev. ed.; Public Record Office, Richmond, Surrey, 1997; xii, 87pp.

(Public Record Office Readers' Guide; no. 3)

ISBN 1-873162-44-8

WHITE, Arthur S

A Bibliography of Regimental Histories of the British Army compiled by Arthur S White with a foreword by Field Marshal Sir Gerald WR Templer.

London Stamp Exchange, London, 1988; viii, 317pp.

ISBN 0-948130-61-X

WISE, Terence

A Guide to Military Museums and Other Places of Military Interest by Terence and Shirley Wise.

10th rev. ed.; Imperial Press, Knighton, Powys, 2001; 90pp.

ISBN 1-85674-035-8

GENERAL BOOKS ABOUT ARMY STRUCTURE, ORGANISATION AND LIFE

The *Army List* is the official publication that lists all officers – some issues have been republished.

BALDWIN, Stanley Simm
Forward Everywhere: Her Majesty's Territorials by Stanley Simm Baldwin.
Brassey's (UK), London, 1994; xxv, 278pp; 24pp of plates; ill., ports.
ISBN 0-08-040716-1

BECKETT, Ian FW
The Amateur Military Tradition, 1558-1945 by Ian FW Beckett.
Manchester University Press, Manchester, 1991; ix, 340pp; ill., facsims.
(Manchester History of the British Army)
ISBN 0-7190-2912-0

CARVER, Michael
Britain's Army in the Twentieth Century by Field Marshal Lord Carver.
Macmillan, London, 1998; xx, 550pp; 70pp of plates; ill., some col., maps, ports.
ISBN 0-333-73777-6

CHANDLER, David
The Oxford Illustrated History of the British Army, General Editor David Chandler, Associate Editor Ian Beckett.
Oxford University Press, Oxford, 1994; xvii, 493pp; 22pp of plates; ill., some col., ports.
ISBN 0-19-869178-5

FREDERICK, JBM

The Lineage Book of British Land Forces 1660-1978: Biographical Outlines of Cavalry, Yeomanry, Armour, Artillery, Infantry, Marines and Air Force Land Troops of the Regular and Reserve Forces compiled by JBM Frederick.

Rev. and enl. ed.; Microform Academic Publishers, East Ardsley, Wakefield, 1984; 2 vols.

ISBN 1-85117-009-X

HALLOWS, Ian S

Regiments and Corps of the British Army by Ian S Hallows.

Arms and Armour Press, London, 1991; 320pp; figs.

ISBN 0-85368-998-9

SWINSON, Arthur

A Register of the Regiments and Corps of the British Army: the Ancestry of the Regiments and Corps of the Regular Establishment edited by Arthur Swinson with a foreword by Lieutenant-General Sir Brian Horrocks.

Archive Press, London, 1972; lix, 339pp.

ISBN 0-85591-000-3

FIRST WORLD WAR

ARTHUR, Max

Forgotten Voices of the Great War by Max Arthur.

Ebury Press, London, 2002; x, 326pp; ill., ports.

Published in association with the Imperial War Museum

ISBN 0-09188209-5

BECKE, AF

Order of Battle of Divisions; parts 1 - 4 compiled by Major AF Becke by direction of the Historical Section of the Committee of Imperial Defence.

HMSO, London, 1935-1945; 6 vols.; ca. 1,100pp in various pagings.

(History of the Great War: Based on Official Documents)

BECKETT, Ian FW

A Nation in Arms: a Social Study of the British Army in the First World War edited by Ian FW Beckett and Keith Simpson.

Manchester University Press, Manchester, 1985; 276pp; ill., map, ports.

ISBN 0-7190-1737-8

BET-EL, Ilana R

Conscripts: Lost Legions of the Great War by Ilana R Bet-El.

Sutton Publishing, Stroud, Gloucestershire, 1999; xv, 239pp; 16pp of plates; ill., facsims.

ISBN 0-7509-2108-0

BROWN, Malcolm

The Imperial War Museum Book of 1914: the Men who went to War by Malcolm Brown.

Sidgwick and Jackson, London, 2004; xxviii, 337pp; 24pp of plates; ill., maps, ports.

ISBN 0-283-07323-3

BROWN, Malcolm

The Imperial War Museum Book of 1918: Year of Victory by Malcolm Brown.

Sidgwick and Jackson, London, 1998; xxxiii, 392pp; 16pp of plates; ill., facsims., maps, ports.

ISBN 0-283-06307-6

BROWN, Malcolm

The Imperial War Museum Book of the First World War: a Great Conflict Recalled in Previously Unpublished Letters, Diaries, Documents and Memoirs by Malcolm Brown.

Sidgwick and Jackson, London, 1991; 288pp; ill., some col., facsims., maps, ports.

ISBN 0-283-99946-2

BROWN, Malcolm
The Imperial War Museum Book of the Somme by Malcolm Brown.
Sidgwick and Jackson, London, 1996; xxxvi, 380pp; 16pp of plates; ill., maps, ports.
ISBN 0-283-06249-5

BROWN, Malcolm
The Imperial War Museum Book of the Western Front by Malcolm Brown.
Sidgwick and Jackson, London, 1993; xiii, 274pp; 8pp of plates; ill., some col., facsims., maps, ports.
ISBN 0-283-061405

BULL, Stephen
World War One: British Army by Stephen Bull, colour plates by Christa Hook.
Brassey's, London, 1998; 144pp; chiefly ill., some col., facsims., figs., ports.
(Brassey's History of Uniforms)
ISBN 1-85753-270-8

COX, Reginald HW
Military Badges of the British Empire, 1914-18 by Reginald HW Cox.
Ernest Benn, London, 1982; 363pp; 4pp of plates; ill., some col., figs.
ISBN 0-510-00082-7

JAMES, EA
British Regiments 1914-1918 by Brigadier EA James, CBE, TD.
Samson Books, London, 1978; 140pp.
ISBN 0-906304-03-2

KIPLING, Arthur L
Head-dress Badges of the British Army by Arthur L Kipling and Hugh L King.
Muller, London, 1973-1979; 2 vols.

MARRION, RJ

The British Army 1914-18 text by RJ Marrion and DSV Foster, colour plates by GA Embleton.

Osprey Publishing, London, 1978; 40pp; ill., 8 col. plates; pbk.

(Men-at-Arms Series edited by Martin Windrow)

ISBN 0-85045-287-2

MESSENGER, Charles

Call to Arms: the British Army 1914-18 by Charles Messenger.

Weidenfeld and Nicholson, London, 2005; 574pp; 16pp of plates; ill.

ISBN 0-297-84695-7

MIDDLEBROOK, Martin

Your Country Needs You: from Six to Sixty-Five Divisions by Martin Middlebrook.

Leo Cooper, Barnsley, South Yorkshire, 2000; 176pp; ill., figs., map, ports.

ISBN 0-85052-711-2

SIMKINS, Peter

Kitchener's Army: the Raising of the New Armies, 1914-16 by Peter Simkins.

Manchester University Press, Manchester, 1988; xvi, 359pp.

(War, Armed Forces and Society)

ISBN 0-7190-26376

WESTLAKE, Ray

The British Army of August 1914: an Illustrated Directory by Ray Westlake.

Spellmount, Staplehurst, Kent, 2005; 192pp; 16pp of plates; ill., figs., ports.

ISBN 1-86227-207-7

WESTLAKE, Ray

British Battalions in France and Belgium, 1914 by Ray Westlake.

Leo Cooper, London, 1997; xxiv, 354pp; 8pp of plates; ill., maps, ports.

ISBN 0-85052-577-2

WESTLAKE, Ray
British Battalions on the Somme, 1916 by Ray Westlake.
Leo Cooper, London, 1994; 308pp; 8pp of plates; ill., facsims., ports.
ISBN 0-85052-374-5

WESTLAKE, Ray
British Regiments at Gallipoli by Ray Westlake.
Leo Cooper, London, 1996; xii, 285pp; 8pp of plates; ill., facsims., maps, ports.
ISBN 0-85052-511-X

WILLIAMSON, Howard
The Collector and Researchers Guide to the War by Howard Williamson.
Anne Williamson, Harwich, Essex, 2003; 2 vols.; ill., facsims., figs., frontis., maps, ports.
ISBN 0-9527544-1-X

WINTER, Denis
Death's Men: Soldiers of the Great War by Denis Winter.
Allen Lane, London, 1978; 283pp; 24pp of plates; ill., ports.
ISBN 0-7139-1068-2

SECOND WORLD WAR

ARTHUR, Max
Forgotten Voices of the Second World War by Max Arthur.
Ebury Press, London, 2004; x, 486pp; ill., ports.
Published in assocation with the Imperial War Museum
ISBN 0-09189734-3

BELLIS, Malcolm A
Brigades of the British Army 1939-45 by MA Bellis.
MA Bellis, Crewe, Cheshire, 1986; 89pp; figs.

BELLIS, Malcolm A

Divisions of the British Army 1939-45 by MA Bellis.

MA Bellis, Crewe, Cheshire, 1986; 83pp; figs.

BELLIS, Malcolm A

Regiments of the British Army 1939-1945: Artillery by MA Bellis.

Military Press International, London, 1995; 123pp.

(British and Foreign Armies World War Two Order of Battle Series; Vol. 2)

ISBN 0-85420-110-6

BELLIS, Malcolm A

21st Army Group Order of Battle compiled by MA Bellis.

MA Bellis, Crewe, Cheshire, 1991; 85pp; ill., figs., maps, plans; pbk.

(Datafile; 8)

ISBN 0-9512126-7-2

BRAYLEY, Martin

The World War II Tommy: British Army Uniforms, European Theatre, 1939-45: in Colour Photographs by Martin Brayley and Richard Ingram.

Crowood Press, Marlborough, Wiltshire, 1998; 144pp; ill.

ISBN 1-86126-190-X

BUTLER, Kenneth W

British Army Orders of Battle, 1939-1945: a Finding List - Supplement to Joslen by Kenneth W Butler and Robert W Lockerby.

Tualatin Plains Press, Portland, Oregon, 1995; v, 544pp.

COLE, Howard N

Formation Badges of World War 2: Britain, Commonwealth and Empire by Howard N Cole.

Arms and Armour Press, London, 1973; 192pp; 4pp of plates; ill.

ISBN 0-85368-078-7

DAVIS, Brian L

British Army Uniforms and Insignia of World War Two by Brian L Davis.
Arms and Armour Press, London, 1983; 276pp; ill., some col., figs., ports.

FORTY, George

British Army Handbook, 1939-1945 by George Forty.
Sutton Publishing, Stroud, Gloucestershire, 1998; xii, 369pp; ill., frontis.,
facsims., figs., ports.
ISBN 0-7509-1403-3

FRASER, David

And We Shall Shock Them: the British Army in the Second World War by David
Fraser.
Hodder and Stoughton, London, 1983; xiii, 429pp; 12pp of plates; ill., maps,
ports.
ISBN 0-340-22085-3

FRENCH, David

*Raising Churchill's Army: the British Army and the War against Germany, 1919-
1945* by David French.
Oxford University Press, Oxford, 2000; xii, 319pp
ISBN 0-19-820641-0

GILBERT, Adrian

The Imperial War Museum Book of the Desert War by Adrian Gilbert.
Sidgwick and Jackson, London, 1992; xv, 208pp; 16pp of plates; ill., maps, plans,
ports.
ISBN 0-283-06129-4

JOSLEN, HF

*Orders of Battle: United Kingdom and Colonial Formations and Units in the Second
World War, 1939-1945 prepared for the Historical Section of the Cabinet Office*
by Lieutenant-Colonel HF Joslen.
HMSO, London, 1960; 2 vols., xii, 628pp.

THOMPSON, Julian

The Imperial War Museum Book of Victory in Europe by Julian Thompson.
Sidgwick and Jackson, London, 1994; xiv, 274pp; ill., frontis., ports, maps.
ISBN 0-283-06161-8

THOMPSON, Julian

The Imperial War Museum Book of War Behind Enemy Lines by Julian
Thompson.
Sidgwick and Jackson, London, 1998; xxxii, 476pp; 24pp of plates; ill., maps,
ports.
ISBN 0-283-06253-3

THOMPSON, Julian

*The Imperial War Museum Book of the War in Burma, 1942-1945: a Vital
Contribution to Victory in the Far East* by Julian Thompson.
Pan Books, London, 2002; xxiv, 456pp; 24pp of plates; ill., maps, ports.
ISBN 0-330-48065-0

UNITED STATES. WAR DEPARTMENT

*Handbook on the British Army 1943: with Supplements on the Royal Air Force and
Civilian Defense Organizations.*
Department of Printed Books, Imperial War Museum, London, 2005; vii,
403pp; ill., figs., plans.
(United States Technical Manual; TM 30-410; Battery Press Reference Series;
no. 24)
ISBN 1-904897-05-3

POST 1945 – NATIONAL SERVICE

BLAXLAND, Gregory
The Regiments Depart: a History of the British Army, 1945-1970 by Gregory
Blaxland.
Kimber, London, 1971; xi, 532pp; maps.
ISBN 0-7183-0012-2

FORTY, George
Called Up: a National Service Scrapbook by George Forty.
Ian Allan, London, 1980; 128pp; chiefly ill., facsims., ports.
ISBN 0-7110-1050-1

HICKMAN, Tom
The Call-Up: a History of National Service by Tom Hickman.
Headline, London, 2004; xx, 364pp; 16pp of plates; ill., facsims., ports.
ISBN 0-7553-1240-6

JOHNSON, BS
All Bull: the National Serviceman edited by BS Johnson.
Quartet Books, London, 1973; 293pp; pbk.
ISBN 0-7043-1002-3

ROYLE, Trevor
The Best Years of their Lives: the National Service Experience 1945-63 by Trevor
Royle.
Michael Joseph, London, 1986; xvii, 288pp; 16pp of plates; ill., ports.
ISBN 0-7181-2459-6

THOMPSON, Julian
*The Imperial War Museum Book of Modern Warfare: British and Commonwealth
Forces at War* by Julian Thompson.
Pan Books, London, 2003; xxii, 376pp; 24pp of plates; ill., maps, ports.
ISBN 0-330-39304-9

MEDALS

CAMPAIGN MEDALS

DUCKERS, Peter
British Campaign Medals, 1914-2000 by Peter Duckers.
Shire Publications, Princes Risborough, Buckinghamshire, 2001; 40pp; ill.; pbk.
(Shire Album; no. 393)
ISBN 0-7478-0515-6

DYMOND, Steve
Researching British Military Medals: a Practical Guide by Steve Dymond.
Crowood Press, Marlborough, Wiltshire, 1999; 143pp; ill., facsims., ports.
ISBN 1-86126-282-5

JOSLIN, EC
British Battles and Medals by EC Joslin, AR Litherland and BT Simpkin.
6th ed.; Spink and Son, London, 1988; viii, 299pp; 4pp of plates; ill., some col.,
figs.
ISBN 0-907605-25-7

WILLIAMSON, HJ
Collecting and Researching the Campaign Medals of the Great War by
HJ Williamson.
Harwich Printing Co., Harwich, Essex, 1989; 80pp.

GALLANTRY AWARDS

The Register of the George Cross
This England Books, Cheltenham, Gloucestershire, 1985; 151pp; ports.
ISBN 0-906324-06-8

The Register of the Victoria Cross
Rev. ed.; This England Books, Cheltenham, Gloucestershire, 1988; 352pp;
ports.
ISBN 0-906324-07-6

ABBOTT, PE
British Gallantry Awards by PE Abbott and JMA Tamplin.
Nimrod Dix, London, 1981; xx, 316pp; ill.

BATE, Christopher K
*For Bravery in the Field: Recipients of the Military Medal: 1919-1939, 1939-1945,
1945-1991* by Christopher K Bate, BA and Martin G Smith.
Bayonet Publications, n.p., 1991; viii, 542pp; 4pp of plates; ill., facsims., map,
port.
ISBN 1-873996-00-4

BROWN, George A
*For Distinguished Conduct in the Field: the Register of the Distinguished Conduct
Medal 1939-1992* by George A Brown.
Western Canadian Distributors, Langley, British Columbia, 1993; 543pp.

CREAGH, O'Moore
*The VC and DSO: a Complete Record of all those Officers, Non-commissioned
Officers and Men of His Majesty's Naval, Military and Air Forces who have been
Awarded these Decorations from the Time of their Institution . . .* edited by the
late Sir O'Moore Creagh (until 1920) and EM Humphris, with a foreword by
Earl Beatty, Earl of Cavan and Sir HM Trenchard.
Standard Art Book, London, 1924; 3 vols.; ports.

CROOK, MJ
The Evolution of the Victoria Cross: a Study in Administrative History by MJ Crook.
Midas Books, Tunbridge Wells, Kent, 1975; 321pp; 9pp of plates; ill., facsims.,
figs., col. frontis., ports.
ISBN 0-85936-041-5

DUCKERS, Peter

British Gallantry Awards, 1855-2000 by Peter Duckers.

Shire Publications, Princes Risborough, Buckinghamshire, 2001; 64pp; ill., facsims., ports.; pbk.

(Shire Album; no. 394)

ISBN 0-7478-0516-4

HARVEY, David

Monuments to Courage: Victoria Cross Headstones and Memorials by David Harvey.

K and K Patience, N.p., 1999; 2 vols.; ill., facsims., figs., ports.

HENDERSON, DV

Dragons can be Defeated: a Complete Record of the George Medal's Progress, 1940-1983 by Major (Ret'd) DV Henderson, GM.

Spink and Son, London, 1984; 120pp.

ISBN 0-90-7605-14-1

KAMARYC, RM

The Military Cross: Awarded to Officers and Warrant Officers from 1937 to 1993 researched and compiled by Lieutenant-Colonel RM Kamaryc.

Concept Colour, Bishop's Stortford, Hertfordshire, 1994; 549pp.

ISBN 0-9518638-2-7

MACKINLAY, GA

Beyond Duty: the Distinguished Conduct Medal to the British Commonwealth of Nations, 1920-1992: and Other Pertinent Awards by Gordon Angus Mackinlay.

James Stedman, Sydney, 1993; vii, 278pp; ill., ports.

ISBN 0-646-16611-5

McDERMOTT, Philip

For Distinguished Conduct in the Field: the Register of the Distinguished Conduct Medal, 1920-1992 compiled by Philip McDermott.

JB Hayward, Polstead, Suffolk, 1994; 2 vols.

McINNES, Ian

The Annuity Meritorious Service Medal, 1847-1953 by Ian McInnes.

Jade Publishing, Oldham, Lancashire, 1995; xxiii, 450pp; 12 leaves of plates; col. ill., facsims., ports.

ISBN 0-9518098-4-9

[this is not a gallantry medal]

McINNES, Ian

The Meritorious Service Medal: the Immediate Awards, 1916-1928 by Ian McInnes.

Naval and Military Press, Dallington, East Sussex, 1992; 511pp; 4pp of plates; facsim., ports.

ISBN 0-948130-74-1

MULHOLLAND, John

Victoria Cross Bibliography by John Mulholland and Alan Jordan.

Spink, London, 1999; xvii, 217pp.

ISBN 1-902040-21-X

WALKER, RW

Recipients of the Distinguished Conduct Medal, 1914-1920: being a List arranged Regimentally and Alphabetically of all those Awarded the DCM between August 1914 and June 1920 compiled by RW Walker.

Midland Medals, Birmingham, 1981; xx, 219pp; 6 ill., 15 ports.

ISBN 0-907455-00-X

WEBB, Jack V

Recipients of Bars to the Military Cross 1916-1920: to which is added MCs to Warrant Officers, 1915-1919 by Jack V Webb.

Jack V Webb, London, 1988; 199pp.

ISBN 0-85421-014-9

ROLLS OF HONOUR

The National Roll of the Great War 1914-1918: Sections I-XIV.

National Publishing, London, 1920-1922?; 14 vols. [plus index]

Officers Died in the Great War, 1914-1919.

HMSO, London, 1919; 262pp.

Soldiers Died in the Great War, 1914-19

HMSO, London, 1921; 80 vols.

BELL, Ernest W

Soldiers Killed on the First Day of the Somme by Ernest W Bell.

W Bell, Bolton, Lancashire, 1977; vi, 212pp.

GASTON, Peter

The Roll of Honour, Malaya 1948-1960 by Peter Gaston.

P Gaston, Chester, 1979; v, 193 leaves.

JARVIS, SD

Cross of Sacrifice. Volume 1: Officers who Died in the Service of British, Indian and East African Regiments and Corps 1914-1919 by SD and DB Jarvis.

Roberts Medals, Reading, 1993; 380pp.

ISBN 1873058-26-8

RUVIGNY, Melville (9th Marquis of Ruvigny and Raineval)
The Roll of Honour: a Biographical Record of all Members of His Majesty's Naval and Military Forces who have Fallen in the War by the Marquis de Ruvigny.
Standard Art Book Company, London, n.d.; ill., ports.
Incomplete set held by IWM.

SUTTON, Malcolm
Bear in Mind these Dead ... : an Index of Deaths from the Conflict in Ireland, 1969-93 edited by Malcolm Sutton.
Beyond the Pale Publications, Belfast, 1994; xi, 226pp; 2 maps, pbk.
ISBN 0-9514229-4-4

WALKER, Rob
To What End did they Die?: Officers Died at Gallipoli by Rob Walker.
RW Walker, Worcester, 1985; xi, 252pp; ill., maps, ports.
ISBN 0-9510608-0-5

WAR OFFICE
United Kingdom Personnel Killed or Died in Korea compiled by the War Office.
N. pub.; War Office, London, n.d.; 41 leaves.

MEDICAL HISTORIES

CREW, FAE
The Army Medical Services. Campaigns by FAE Crew.
HMSO, London, 1956-1966; 5 vols.; ill., maps.
(History of the Second World War: United Kingdom Medical Series)

MACPHERSON, WG
Medical Services. General History by Major-General Sir WG Macpherson.
HMSO, London, 1921-1924; 4 vols.; ill., figs., maps.
(History of the Great War: Based on Official Documents)

WHITEHEAD, Ian R
Doctors in the Great War by Ian R Whitehead.
Leo Cooper, Barnsley, South Yorkshire, 1999; x, 309pp; 12pp of plates; ill.
ISBN 0-85052-691-4

TRENCH MAPS

CHASSEAUD, Peter
Topography of Armageddon: a British Trench Map Atlas of the Western Front, 1914-1918 by Peter Chasseaud, preface by Alan Sillitoe.
Mapbooks, Lewes, East Sussex, 1991; 200pp; maps; pbk.
ISBN 0-9512080-1-2

CHASSEAUD, Peter
Trench Maps: a Collectors' Guide by Peter Chasseaud.
Mapbooks, Lewes, East Sussex, 1986; 56pp; maps.
(British Regular Series 1:10,000 Trench Maps GSGS 3062; Vol. 1)

BATTLEFIELD GUIDES

Leo Cooper is publishing a series called *Battleground Europe* which consists of paperbacks covering particular battlefields, often in great detail, and taking a broad definition of 'Europe'. The magazine *After the Battle* is also extremely useful, looking at places in a 'then and now' context.

COOMBS, Rose EB
Before Endeavours Fade: a Guide to the Battlefields of the First World War by Rose EB Coombs.
4th ed.; Battle of Britain Prints International, London, 1983; 160pp; ill., maps, plans, ports.; pbk. An After the Battle publication.
ISBN 0-900913-27-4

HOLMES, Richard

Army Battlefield Guide: Belgium and Northern France by Richard Holmes.
HMSO, London, 1995; xi, 222pp; 16pp of plates; ill., maps, ports.; pbk.
ISBN 0-11-772762-8

HOLT, Tonie

Major and Mrs Holt's Battlefield Guide to Gallipoli by Tonie and Valmai Holt.
Leo Cooper, Barnsley, South Yorkshire, 2000; 272pp; ill., map, plan, ports.; pbk.
ISBN 0-85052-638-8

HOLT, Tonie

Major and Mrs Holt's Battlefield Guide to the Normandy Landing Beaches by
Tonie and Valmai Holt.
Leo Cooper, Barnsley, South Yorkshire, 1999; 272pp; ill., some col., facsims.,
maps, plans; pbk.
ISBN 0-85052-662-0

HOLT, Tonie

Major and Mrs Holt's Battlefield Guide to the Somme by Tonie Holt and Valmai
Holt.
Leo Cooper, London, 1996; 254pp; ill., chiefly col., maps; pbk.
ISBN 0-85052-414-8

HOLT, Tonie

Major and Mrs Holt's Battlefield Guide to the Ypres Salient by Tonie and Valmai
Holt.
3rd ed.; Leo Cooper, London, 2000; 256pp; ill., chiefly col., maps, ports.; pbk.
ISBN 0-85052-551-9

KEUNG, Ko Tim

Ruins of War: a Guide to Hong Kong's Battlefields and Wartime Sites by Ko Tim
Keung and Jason Wordie.
Joint Publishing, Hong Kong, 1996; 214pp; chiefly ill., maps, plans; pbk.
ISBN 962-04-1372-5

MIDDLEBROOK, Martin
The Somme Battlefields: a Comprehensive Guide from Crecy to the Two World Wars by Martin and Mary Middlebrook.
Viking, London, 1991; xii, 385pp; ill., figs., maps, ports.
ISBN 0-670-83083-6

MILITARY WIVES AND CHILDREN

BAMFIELD, Veronica
On the Strength: the Story of the British Army Wife by Veronica Bamfield.
Knight, London, 1974; 223pp; ill., ports.
ISBN 0-85314-231-9

WILLIAMS, Noel T St John
Tommy Atkins' Children: the Story of the Education of the Army's Children, 1675-1970 by Colonel NT St John Williams.
HMSO, London, 1971; xv, 251pp; 32pp of plates; ill., frontis., ports.

WILLIAMS, Noel T St John
Judy O'Grady and the Colonel's Lady: the Army Wife and Camp Follower since 1660 by Colonel Noel T St John Williams.
Brassey's Defence, London, 1988; xii, 269pp; 28pp of plates; ill., facsims., frontis., maps, ports.
ISBN 0-08-035826-8

RESEARCH FACILITIES AT THE IMPERIAL WAR MUSEUM

THE READING ROOM

Formerly the chapel of the Bethlem Royal Hospital, or Bedlam, this historic room is used extensively by authors, scholars, journalists, broadcasters and visitors alike. Readers have access to a major reference library of printed materials encompassing everything from trench maps to a vast journals collection. The Department of Documents holds an extensive collection of unpublished diaries, letters and memoirs of servicemen and women and civilians.

Access to the Reading Room is free but you should make an appointment in advance.

Monday – Saturday 10.00am-5.00pm
Closed: Bank Holiday weekends, 24, 25, 26 December and for a period of 2 weeks (usually May) for stocktaking purposes

When making an appointment please give us as much detail of your area of research as possible. Material can then be pre-selected and ready on your arrival. However, this should not deter you from a further catalogue search of your own. We will be happy to show you the various catalogues and options open to you. Bags are not generally allowed in the reading room – these should be left in the cloakroom – although handbags and portable computers are admissible. Please remember that this is an old building and, although we have done much to improve the provision of electric points, lighting and ventilation, we are limited by the amount of physical space actually available. We will, however, always try to accommodate anyone wishing to consult our collections. The design limitations of this building make access to the Reading Room difficult for many disabled visitors but alternative facilities are available. Please ask when making your appointment.

Photocopying and other services

Guidance on photocopying procedures is available in printed form in the Reading Room itself. We are bound by the copyright law, and by our own conservation and preservation requirements. Black and white photocopies are available at a fixed Museum price and special photography can be arranged. Booklists and information sheets are available on a variety of subjects.

Our contact details:

Department of Printed Books
Imperial War Museum, Lambeth Road, London SE1 6HZ
Tel: 020 7416 5342 (for general enquiries and appointments)
Fax: 020 7416 5246
E-mail: books@iwm.org.uk

Department of Documents
Imperial War Museum, Lambeth Road, London SE1 6HZ
Tel: 020 7416 5222
Fax: 020 7416 5374
E-mail: docs@iwm.org.uk

Other Collecting Departments
[all postal enquiries should be addressed to the appropriate department at Imperial War Museum, Lambeth Road, London SE1 6HZ]

Department of Art
Material may be seen by prior appointment in the Print Room at the Museum's Lambeth Road branch, Tuesday-Thursday, 10.00am-5.00pm. To arrange a visit, contact the Department's Research and Information Officer.
Tel: 020 7416 5211
E-mail: art@iwm.org.uk

Department of Exhibits and Firearms
A visitor's room is open by appointment, Monday-Friday, 10.00am-5.00pm.
Tel: 020 7416 5308
Fax: 020 7416 5374
E-mail: exfire@iwm.org.uk

Film and Photograph Archives

The Film Archive is open by appointment from Monday-Friday, 10.00am-5.00pm. At least 24 hours notice is normally sufficient to research the catalogue, but 5-7 days notice is required to view any film selected. Film viewing and handling fees are charged. The Visitor's Room is located at: All Saints Annexe, Austral Street, London SE11.
Tel: 020 7416 5291 / 5292
Fax: 020 7416 5299
E-mail: film@iwm.org.uk

The Photograph Archive Visitors' Room at the All Saints Annexe, Austral Street, is open to visitors, by appointment, from Monday-Friday, 10.00am-5.00pm.
Tel: 020 7416 5333 / 5338 [Please allow a minimum of 24 hours notice]
Fax: 020 7416 5355
E-mail: photos@iwm.org.uk

Sound Archive

The Visitors Room at the All Saints Annexe, Austral Street is open by appointment, Monday to Friday, 10.00am-5.00pm. Visitors may listen to tapes and consult printed and database catalogues; some typescripts available.
Tel: 020 7416 5363
E-mail: sound@iwm.org.uk

Collections Online

An exciting new development has been the launch of **Collections Online** at **www.iwmcollections.org.uk**
The initial tranche of material was made public in 2002, and catalogues from all the Collecting Departments were made

available in 2004. For the first time you can access the Museum's catalogues online. If you want to browse there are short essays on major historical themes, which lead you to selected highlights from all over the collections, including artworks, documents, exhibits, film, photographs and sound recordings. Currently 160,000 records are available, although it is important to realise that no catalogue is ever totally complete – if you don't find what you are looking for, please contact us and ask.

GENERAL CONTACTS

The Museum has five branches. These are:

Imperial War Museum London
Lambeth Road, London SE1 6HZ
Open daily, 10.00am-6.00pm
Tel: 020 7416 5320 / 5321 (general enquiries)
Fax: 020 7416 5374
E-mail: mail@iwm.org.uk

Churchill Museum and Cabinet War Rooms
Clive Steps, King Charles Street, London SW1A 2AQ
Open daily
Summer (1 April-30 September) 9.30am-6.00pm
last admission 5.15pm
Winter 10.00am-6.00pm, last admission 5.15pm
Tel: 020 7930 6961
Fax: 020 7839 5897
E-mail: cwr@iwm.org.uk

HMS *Belfast*
Morgan's Lane, Tooley Street, London SE1 2JH
Open daily
Summer (1 March-31 October) 10.00am-6.00pm,
last admission 5.15pm
Winter 10.00am-5.00pm, last admission 4.15pm
Tel: 020 7940 6300
Fax: 020 7403 0719
E-mail: hmsbelfast@iwm.org.uk

Imperial War Museum Duxford
Cambridgeshire CB2 4QR
Open daily
Summer (mid March-mid October) 10.00am-6.00pm,
last admission 5.15pm
Winter 10.00am-4.00pm, last admission 3.15pm
Tel: 01223 835000
Fax: 01223 837267
E-mail: duxford@iwm.org.uk

Imperial War Museum North
The Quays, Trafford Wharf, Trafford Park,
Manchester M17 1TZ
Open daily
Summer (1 March-31 October) 10.00am-6.00pm,
last admission 5.30pm
Winter 10.00am-5.00pm, last admission 4.30pm
Tel: 0161 836 4000
Fax: 0161 836 4012
E-mail: iwmnorth@iwm.org.uk

All branches are closed 24, 25, 26 December

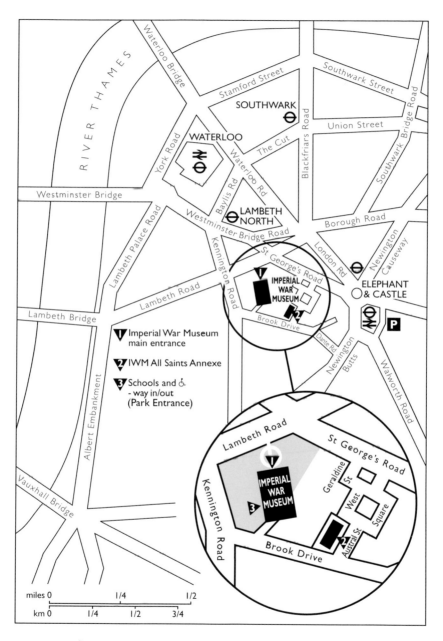

Map labels

RIVER THAMES

Waterloo Bridge

Stamford Street

SOUTHWARK

Southwark Street

Southwark Bridge Road

WATERLOO

York Road

Bayliss Rd

Waterloo Rd

The Cut

Blackfriars Road

Union Street

Westminster Bridge

Lambeth Palace Road

Westminster Bridge Road

LAMBETH NORTH

Borough Road

London Rd

Newington Causeway

ELEPHANT & CASTLE

Lambeth Road

Kennington Road

St George's Road

IMPERIAL WAR MUSEUM

Brook Drive

Lambeth Bridge

Dante Rd

Newington Butts

P

Walworth Road

Albert Embankment

▼ Imperial War Museum main entrance

❷ IWM All Saints Annexe

❸ Schools and ♿ - way in/out (Park Entrance)

Vauxhall Bridge

Lambeth Road

St George's Road

Kennington Road

IMPERIAL WAR MUSEUM

Geraldine St

West Square

Brook Drive

Austral St

	miles 0	1/4	1/2	
km 0	1/4	1/2	3/4	

www.iwm.org.uk